- Patients using kidney dialysis machines . . .

- Those who may be allergic to chlorine and fluoride . . .

- Arthritics who are prone to mineral deposits . . .

- Men and women of all ages who discovered astonishing new health and vigor . . .

> All have one thing in common—the discovery of their own need for *pure water*. And here, in this updated, original book, a respected authority shows the reasons why your body needs pure water and tells you the simple way to assure

### Your Water and Your Health

## Keats titles of related interest

# YOUR WATER AND YOUR HEALTH

Revised 1990 Edition

Dr. Allen E. Banik
with Carlson Wade

Keats Publishing, Inc. New Canaan, Connecticut

*"Man has lost the capacity to foresee and to
  forestall.
He will end by destroying the earth."*
                                    **Albert Schweitzer**

YOUR WATER AND YOUR HEALTH

Pivot Original Health Book published June, 1974
Revised editions published in 1981, 1990.

Printed in the United States of America

Library of Congress Cataloging-in-Publication Data

Banik, Allen E.
    Your water and your health / Allen E. Banik with Carlson
Wade.—Rev. ed.
      p.     cm.
    ISBN: 0-87983-514-1
    1. Drinking water—Health aspects.  2. Drinking water—
Contamination  3. Water—Pollution—Toxicology.  4. Water,
Distilled.  I. Wade, Carlson.  II. Title.
RA591.836   1990
613'.3—dc20                                                    90-4821
                                                                  CIP

Keats Publishing, Inc.
27 Pine Street (Box 876)
New Canaan, Connecticut 06840

## MY GRATITUDE TO:

To: *Luke Thomas,* who spent hours going over my manuscript. His kindly advice and missionary spirit have become a part of this book.

To: *Eldon C. Muehling,* author of *Water for the Eighties; A Cause for Concern.* His inspiration kept me going.

To: *My son-in-law, Dr. Wm. Zeigler,* who kept our Vision Clinic operating during my two-year absence.

To: *My wife Elane,* who spent solitary nights, while I remained in seclusion.

To: *(Miss) Peg Austin,* journalist, typist, whose keen mind remembered every detail. To all my readers, I wish you—health!

Allen E. Banik, O.D.

Dr. Allen E. Banik is a man America ought to get to know. He knows more about water and what polluted water will do in the physiological mechanism than more professionals alive on this *globe* today.

Dr. Banik has written this book to help you understand the relation of polluted water to your health and diet, and subsequently the health of our nation. As you plan the future of your children don't overlook the science of nutrition and the physical body. Learn the facts; become aware of the truth and build a strong, healthy America.

CHUCK WALTERS, *Editor*
ACRES, U.S.A.

# Contents

## DID YOU KNOW?

- Did you know that more than 25,000 people die each day around the world from disease caused by dirty water or no water at all! (That's about 90 million people annually!)
- Did you know that the absence of clean drinking water and sanitation is one of the biggest causes of death and loss of human productivity throughout the world?
- Did you know that three to four of every five children in the world die because of polluted water diseases such as dysentery, cholera and malaria?

# CHAPTER 1

# *Pollution in Your Drinking Water*

Community water utilities realize that they are in a new world of mounting pollution as the problems of supplying safe, clean water grow in quality and quantity.

About 75 percent of our water, for domestic and agricultural use, comes from the earth's surface—from lakes, rivers and reservoirs. This water is pumped up from underground and then stored in the form of wells. It is known as ground water, and it is subject to pollution as a result of what is known as "overdrafts." These occur when coastal fresh water levels are low, and therefore polluted sea water seeps into the storage wells. This leads to forms of municipal sewage in these well waters.

Another major source of pollution in our domestic wells can be traced to the dumping of untreated or insufficiently treated sewage into our waterways. We all know that in many communities, everything—all waste—goes down the same drain—domestic wastes, industrial waste, storm sewer drainage from run-off, and so on. Such wastes may or may not go through a sewage treatment plant, which means that this polluted disposal, untreated, seeps into our stored well water, thus affecting the water you take from your tap for drinking, bathing and other home purposes.

Pollution of our waterways therefore becomes a matter of growing concern as thousands of new chemicals find their way into our raw water sources; and keeping water safe in the midst of this increasing pollution, urbanization and rapidly growing population has become a task beset with what appears to be overwhelming problems.

The majority of the nation's water treatment plants are obsolete. They were engineered to cope with the water problems of a half-century and more ago. Their primary objectives at the time of installation were to cope with the dangers of bacteria and suspended solids. They are incapable of solving the problems arising from dangerous chemicals, viruses and metals now present in available source waters.

Water treatment experts are in agreement that the pollution problem has and is mounting with such intensity that municipal facilities and their piping facilities, now and in the foreseeable future, cannot deliver water acceptable for domestic use, and that this job will have to be done in the home. The solution proposes three types of water: 1. Raw water to be used for outside irrigation and cleaning; 2. Conditioned water for laundry and other inside cleaning; 3. Pure water for drinking and cooking. It is agreed that the only certain, feasible, economic solution to your conditioned and pure water needs is to provide for them in the house or apartment.

One of the principal obstacles in municipal water problems, obviously, is that of proper, constant supervision which unfortunately costs money. It is because of the lack of proper funding that many state health departments no longer have the personnel or equipment to make the necessary checks for appropriate pollution control or to make them on any kind of frequency basis.

Politics in many instances is a controlling factor, stemming largely from the fact that almost 80 percent of our water utilities are municipally owned, which means that they are subject to political controls which relate rate structures to votes rather than costs; and that tie water revenues to supporting the municipality and its political structure rather than dedicating such revenues to improved water service for the benefit of those who actually pay for it. When you get right down to it, a water department is a water utility. It can take care of itself if left to do so. Unfortunately, too often it is not.

*How safe is your drinking water?* For truly

good health, you should have at your disposal safe, pure drinking water. You may think you are getting this every time you open your tap at home, but this is not always the case.

### Tap water: More than just $H_2O$

Chemistry students know that a water molecule consists of two hydrogen atoms and one oxygen atom. But in many communities nationwide, water—from municipal sources and wells—contains more than that. With increasing frequency, trace metals (some of which may be toxic), sodium and other contaminants are finding their way into America's drinking water through such processes as pipe corrosion, water softening and particle-removal procedures.

*Pipe corrosion.* Corrosion of pipes can cause an increase in the concentration of toxic trace metals in water that passes through them. In this way, cadmium, chromium, cobalt, copper, iron, lead, manganese, nickel, silver and zinc in abnormal amounts can leach from the pipes of the distribution system and dissolve into the finished drinking water.

*Toxic Metals.* The amount and kinds of toxic metals leached from pipes depend upon the type of plumbing materials and service lines used and by the acidity of the water in a particular water distribution system. Moreover, acidic rainwater can increase the acidity of some lake, river and well water, thus making treated tap water from these sources more acidic and more likely to contribute to the leaching of metals. The toxic effects of these metals are well documented. We are discovering more contaminants and more health effects from toxic metals as our measurement methods improve.

*Water treatment.* Many water treatment plants use compounds containing sodium to "soften" hard water. The two processes which contribute the largest amounts of sodium to the raw water are ion exchange softening and lime-soda ash softening. During the softening process, calcium and magnesium (which makes water "hard") are removed and replaced with sodium. The higher the hardness of the raw water, the more sodium is required to soften it. Ion exchange softening results in sodium concentration of 70 to 340 milligrams per liter (mg/l), and the level for lime soda ash softening is 30 to 200 mg/l—both substantially greater levels than the 20/mg/l recommended by the Environmental Protection Agency and the American Heart Association.

For infants, the American Academy of Pediatrics recommends no more than 350 milligrams of sodium per day. In areas where water is softened, this recommended amount could easily go over the limit by lunchtime, given the water used in formulas, juices and for cooking.

*Sodium in water.* Other processes that contribute small amounts of sodium to raw water are: disinfection with sodium hypochlorite; pH adjustment with sodium hydroxide or sodium carbonate; and coagulation with sodium silicate or sodium aluminate. In addition, road salt run-off can increase the levels of sodium found in private wells. If you live in communities where water is softened, be aware that the sodium content of your tap water may exceed the recommended 20 mg/l.

*Aluminum in water.* Aluminum is another contaminant found in many water distribution systems. Compounds containing aluminum are frequently added to source water (from lakes, rivers, wells) to remove finely suspended particles. For many years, aluminum was thought to be non-toxic, but there is current evidence of its toxicity to certain cells in the central nervous system. The American Water Works Association has set a guidance level of 50 micrograms per liter for aluminum concentration in drinking water.

### What's in your drinking water?

When you draw a glassful from your tap, you are most likely getting water along with toxic chemicals that could be detrimental to your health. In a report from September 1988 Surgeon General C. Everett Koop, M.D., said:

At high levels, which scientists define as 80 or more micrograms of lead per deciliter of blood, lead poisoning can cause coma, convulsions and death. At half that amount, it can cause permanent damage to the brain and central nervous system, perhaps resulting in amnesia and retardation and interfering with the synthesis of vital blood products, vitamin D and calcium.

The more scientists investigate lead, the more they are seeing its effects at lower and lower concentrations, even as low as 10 micrograms per deciliter. Levels once thought safe are considered safe no longer.

Exposure to lead is particularly hazardous for young children, "because their systems absorb lead more readily than do the systems of adults and because, unlike adults, they are unable to store lead in their bones.

Instead, the lead that young children ingest and absorb goes directly to their vital organs. And because lead crosses the placenta, which means that it moves freely from the body of a pregnant woman into the body of her unborn child, the human fetus can be badly damaged, just as its delicate nervous system is being formed.

The Federal Government has done quite a bit to limit human exposure to lead. Lead-based paint was banned in 1977 by the Consumer Product Safety Commission. The Environmental Protection Agency has reduced the use of leaded gasoline. It also has limited industrial, airborne emissions of lead and it is working to lower lead levels in drinking water. Starting with 1988, lead pipes and lead solder can no longer be used in connection with public water supplies.

The upshot is that while we have made progress in reducing the average level of lead exposure in this country, the problem remains; the more we study it, the more we learn about it, and the more we realize that it is much greater than we previously thought.

It behooves all of us—from physicians and public health workers to teachers and, especially, parents, to keep ourselves and each other fully informed about this toxic and ever-changing threat and to make certain that our children are not being exposed in their varied and daily environments—in nurseries, day care facilities and schools, in public housing, community playgrounds, and even in our own back yards. Young lives are depending on our vigilance.

### *In the news: Contaminated water*

Do these headlines look all too familiar and frightening?

LEAKING STORAGE TANKS THREAT TO UNDERGROUND WATER SUPPLIES.—*Washington Post*.

EPA GROUND WATER PROTECTION RULES CALLED INADEQUATE.—*New York Times*.

U.S. TOXIC CLEANUP MAY TAKE 50 YEARS AND $100 BILLION.—*San Francisco Chronicle*.

STUDY SAYS PESTICIDES CONTAMINATING GROUND WATER.—*Contra Costa Times*.

If you are the least bit unsure about the quality of your drinking water, you need to be alert to the dangers of contaminants.

### *Water contaminants fall into three general categories*

*Inorganics*. More commonly recognized as

minerals, these are composed of anything other than living matter. Local geological conditions determine the natural mineral makeup of water. Minerals may contribute to the taste of water.

*Natural organics.* These come from living matter (decaying plants, sediment, dirt, particulates, bacteria, amoebic cysts and protozoa). These contaminants may contribute to unpleasant taste, color and odor in water and may lead to intestinal disorders.

*Synthetic organics.* Man-made chemicals include urban, agricultural and industrial pollutants such as DBCP, TCE, PCB, etc., as well as chlorine and its by-products. These chemicals react with each other and with natural organics and can create a variety of health problems.

### A closer look at water contaminants

*Particulates.* Suspended particles such as dirt, rust and algae may cloud your drinking water.

*Bacteria/cysts.* Bacteria from human and animal waste and decaying plants; also virus and giardia cysts, which are more resistant to chlorine.

*EPA priority pollutants.* The EPA recognizes 129 toxic "priority pollutants" as posing the greatest threat to drinking water.

*Chlorine.* A common chemical contaminant that kills bacteria and viruses also combines with naturally occurring organics to form chlorinated hydrocarbons known as trihalomethanes

(THMs). These compounds are known cancer-causing substances.

*Urban chemicals.* Gasoline and oils, fertilizers, herbicides and pesticides enter the water system through penetration or run-off.

*Agricultural chemicals.* Herbicides, insecticides and pesticides protect crops and increase our food supply, but toxic chemicals like DDT and EDB mix with irrigation water, permeate the soil and can enter your water supply.

*Industrial chemicals.* Over 100,000 chemical compounds, including PCB, asbestos and solvents, are disposed of in rivers, ponds, landfills and lagoons and create extensive groundwater contamination.

*Heavy toxic metals.* Industrial chemicals and wastes may include toxic heavy metals such as cadmium, lead, arsenic and mercury. Furthermore, acid rain falls on our reservoirs; pesticides and other contaminants seep into our rivers, lakes and wells. The Environmental Protection Agency admits that there are at least 28,000 hazardous waste sites in the U.S., which are potential contaminators of our drinking water.

*The lead problem:* The EPA estimates that 40 million Americans are drinking water which has dangerous lead levels. This is one of the most insidious threats we have ever faced in our tap water. Lead is colorless, odorless, completely undetectable except by professional testing, yet it can seriously damage the brain, kidneys, nervous system and red blood cells.

Those at severe risk are pregnant women, young children and sometimes hyperactive men. The worst aspect of the lead threat is that it occurs after the water has been tested for safety, developing in the pipes that bring it to your house. One study shows that 73 percent of public water systems have lead pipes and 98 percent of home water pipes have lead-soldered joints. If your water proves to have a dangerous lead level, only a very expensive filtration system will correct it; ordinary faucet filters are not effective.

### Poisons in your drinking water

Infectious diseases transmitted through tap water afflict at least thousands of people a year, probably more, since many illnesses such as intestinal "flu" are not seen as to water, though in fact they are. A far more serious threat faces your health. Studies have shown that the nation's 50,000 water supplies are heavily polluted with such harmful substances as asbestos, pesticides, heavy metals including lead, cadmium, arsenic; also nitrates, sodium, viruses and organic chemicals directly linked to cancer.

*The chlorine backlash.* It is ironic that a process purported to cleanse our water of infectious organisms—chlorination—is a double-edged sword because it also creates cancer-causing substances; these are carcinogens that combine with water pollutants to form: chloroform, carbon tetrachloride, bis-chloroethane and other chemicals known as trihalomethanes. Chlorine may well be a killer in disguise.

*Water chemicals and cancer.* At least 300 different organic chemicals have been identified in American drinking water, yet most of them have not been subjected to needed tests for being carcinogens. These chemicals are often present in tiny amounts, but since the average person consumes about one-and-a-half or more quarts of water every day, even small amounts of carcinogens can add up to a potential hazard.

The Environmental Protection Agency via its Safe Drinking Water department, has come up with these findings:

In New Orleans, where the Mississippi River drains agricultural chemicals into the water supply, there is a hazard of chlorinated carcinogens recognized; in this region, cancers of the kidney, bladder and urinary tract are more frequent than in other parts of the country.

A survey of 88 Ohio counties showed that the fatality rates for stomach and bladder cancer were more common among those who were recipients of surface water supplies (from rivers and lakes) than in those who were served with ground water (from wells).

The EPA discovered that organic chemicals are considerably more concentrated in surface water supplies. Furthermore, it was observed that there is a relationship between the levels of trihalomethanes in drinking water and fatalities from cancers of the bladder, brain, kidney and lymph glands.

From the above, it appears there is much cause for concern about a possible waterborne cancer hazard. One way to help reduce this risk is to have the water filtered through active carbon granules before receiving chlorine. But only a few water systems are equipped to do this and it is usually only to remove unpleasant odors and tastes. An alternative method is to use ozone instead of chlorine for water purification.

### Water contaminants that spell health risks

Water that comes from your tap is most likely to contain one or more of these contaminants:

*Nitrates*. These are chemicals already identified in both surface and well water. They enter through agricultural runoff and seepage from septic tanks. Nitrates are especially dangerous to infants, causing blue baby syndrome or methemoglobinemia. For persons of all ages, they may set off the formation of potent carcinogens called nitrosamines in the digestive region. Nitrates can be eliminated from the water supply through an ion exchange process.

*Sodium*. The Environmental Defense Fund has alerted the EPA to initiate stronger water safety measures; they note that a typical water supply may have up to 500 parts of sodium per million parts of water. In certain regions, such as the Northeast and Middle west, sodium overload is seasonal, caused by runoff from highways that have been treated with salt during the winter. In other regions, the water shows very high sodium levels the year round. Excessive salt presents a problem for those who are predisposed to high blood pressure or already have this condition and/or cardiovascular disorders. Although sodium is difficult to remove from water, it would be prudent for the EPA to monitor content periodically and alert the public if there are high levels in the water.

*Metal deposits.* If your area has "soft" water—that is, corrosive water which has rather few dissolved minerals and salts—you face a problem of toxic metals from water pipes leaching into water you draw from the tap. It has been found that there are more deaths from cardiovascular diseases in "soft" water areas than "hard" water areas. It is believed that this may be caused from higher levels of cadmium (leached from galvanized pipes) and sodium in the soft water and lower levels of magnesium, calcium, etc. Some areas, Boston is typical, have lead pipes in the homes; if lime and carbonates are added to the water supply, there is a lowering of its corrosive response.

*Asbestos.* This chemical enters the water supplies mostly through erosion of asbestos-containing rocks and asbestos-cement water pipes as well as run off from roads that have been sanded. Residents drinking water from Lake Superior were reported to have large amounts of asbestos fibers which were traced to dumping from a mining company. There is initial research about the hazards of asbestos in water to show that, for example, asbestos workers exposed to the fibers have very high rates of cancers of the lung and gastrointestinal tract. Asbestos fibers have also been linked to a fatal cancer called mesothelioma. It is possible to reduce asbestos levels in water by hardening the water so it is not too corrosive. Filtration devices can often remove asbestos fibers.

*Radon.* This naturally occurring radioactive gas is formed from uranium and is found everywhere in the crust of the earth. The EPA estimates that inhaled radon causes as many as 40,000 lung-cancer deaths yearly. These occur because radon accumulates in houses after seeping up from the earth and entering through cracks and holes in the foundation. A certain percentage of deaths are attributed to radon from drinking water. The EPA's Office of Drinking Water says that "waterborne radon may cause more cancer deaths than all other drinking water contaminants combined." The EPA further estimates that at least 8 million people have undesirably high radon levels in their water supply. Radon is traced in water from private wells and also to community water systems serving fewer than 500 people. Larger water systems will probably provide some kind of water treatment that aerates the water and disperses radon gas. If you get your drinking water from lakes, reservoirs or rivers, you have little radon worries. (Radon bubbles out before it reaches your faucets.)

"Danger spots" for water-laced radon would include New England (notably Maine, Connecticut, New Hampshire), North Carolina and Arizona. What are the levels that would be a matter of dispute? If your level is 10,000 picocuries per liter or higher, you should be concerned. A level of 10,000 picocuries in water is estimated to release 1 picocurie in indoor air.

If you have levels below 10,000 picocuries, it would be prudent to reduce the radon infiltrating from the ground.

*Reducing exposure to waterborne radon.* In some situations, all you need to do is ventilate your laundry, kitchen or bathroom. Otherwise, you may need to use a water treatment process if you have water from a private well. To remove radon, you need to treat all water coming into your home, not only tap water. One method is to install granular activated carbon units and home aerators. The carbon unit is similar to a water-softener tank and is said to reduce waterborne radon levels by 90 percent. The home aerator is a tank usually installed in the basement. It pumps in air to agitate the water and cause the radon to bubble off. A pipe then vents the gas to the outside.

*Carbon chemicals.* Also known as organic chemicals, they are found in many public water supplies. Organic chemicals are created as byproducts of water chlorination. There is some evidence that these byproducts contain trihalomethanes and may be involved in the risk of cancer. The EPA has no set limits for these

THMs in small water supply systems because such systems have been connected to disease outbreaks from inadequate chlorination. The EPA directs water supply systems serving more than 10,000 residents to keep THM levels below 100 parts per billion. Yet your drinking water may show higher levels!

## WHAT LIES AHEAD

*Water treatment plants have not been designed to get out many trace metals and new chemicals now found in water. And techniques to find out if all viruses have been eliminated from treated water don't exist.*

# CHAPTER 2

## What Can We Do for Better Drinking Water?

Recognition of the widespread need for pure water began to sweep the country when the alarming facts were discovered that deadly pollutants had contaminated our waters. Fish began dying of unknown causes. Diseases such as hepatitis, cholera, salmonella, polio, tetanus and countless viruses deadly to humans began to be traced to water pollution. A concerned Congress worked to appropriate billions of dollars to clean up public water supplies, but purification would still take years. A knowledgeable member of Congress cried out,

"Our tap water is unfit for human consumption. Rubbish is burying the same civilization that produced it."

Researchers soon offered one solution to the problem. It was quick and direct and did not have to be circumvented by years of battles with laws to keep the waterways clean. It consisted of *pure water* being made "instantly" available from every single water tap.

Authorities explained that pure water was a "miracle" because it was disease-free, inorganic mineral-free, chemical-free. It could well be called water fit for the gods to drink; perhaps it was the same water of which Ponce de Leon dreamed but never discovered. Water that would help boost and nourish health. Water which has had removed from it contaminates and substances which the body is unable to use such as: alkyl benzene, alum, arsenic, cadmium, carbon, chlorine, chloroform, chromium, copper, cyanide, fluoride, herbicides, iron, lead, manganese, mercury, nitrate, pesticides, phenols, rust, silver, sulfate, sulfonate, sulfur, zinc and bacteriological radioactive fallout. And this is only a *partial* list. It should be mentioned that chromium, copper, iron, maganese, sulfur and zinc are essential trace minerals; we cannot live without them. However, when they turn up in abnormal amounts in drinking water, air pollution, etc., they can pose a serious health threat.

### The ten kinds of water

Here is a listing of the ten basic kinds of water:

1. HARD WATER. This is saturated with calcium, iron, magnesium and many other inorganic minerals. All water in lakes, rivers, on the ground, in deep wells, is classified as hard

water. (Many city systems take water from rivers or lakes or reservoirs supplied with mountain water; they erroneously call their supplies "soft water" but it is soft only in comparison with water which is harder.)

2. BOILED WATER. Boiling helps remove some of the germs, but concentrates the inorganic minerals. Other germs are carried into a fertile element for rapid and lusty propagation of germs and viruses already in the body.

3. RAW WATER. This has not been boiled. Raw water may be hard (as calcium-hardened water) or soft as rain water. It contains millions of germs and viruses in every densely inhabited drop. Some of these viruses and bacteria may adversely affect the thyroid gland, the liver and other vital body organs.

4. RAIN WATER. This has been condensed from the clouds. The first drop is distilled water. But when it falls as rain, it picks up germs, dust, smoke, minerals, strontium 90, lead and many other atmospheric chemicals. By the time rain water reaches earth it is so saturated with dust and pollutants it may be yellowish in color. Water is supposed to act as an atmosphere purifier. If we had *no* air pollution, we would have far less pollution in our drinking water.

5. SNOW WATER. This is frozen rain. Freezing does not eliminate any germs. All snowflakes have hardened mineral deposits. Melt the cleanest snow and you will find it satu-

rated with dirt, inorganic minerals, germs and viruses.

6. FILTERED WATER. This water has passed through a fine strainer, called a filter. Some calcium and other solid substances are kept in the filter; there is no filter made which can prevent germs from passing through its fine meshes. Each pore of the finest filter is large enough for a million viruses to seep through in a few moments. A home filter usually only picks up suspended solids and is effective for the time, maybe only for hours, until it is filled up. Then it is ineffective even for removing suspended solids, and, at the same time, becomes a breeding ground for bacteria.

7. SOFT WATER. This water is soft in comparison with water which is harder. It may contain many trace minerals and chemicals, viruses and bacteria. It is not to be confused with "softened water." Soft water may be classified as water which is harder than distilled water.

8. REVERSE OSMOSIS. This is a system of water purification which allows pre-filtered water to be forced through a semi-permeable membrane to separate impurities from our drinking water. However, this membrane allows only certain molecules to pass through providing the water pressure is exactly constant. The matter of water pressure is a problem still to be solved. Furthermore, the membrane also allows some iron and nitrate molecules to pass through. Another problem to be solved.

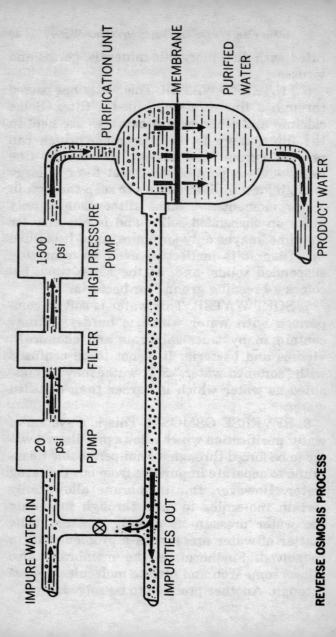

REVERSE OSMOSIS PROCESS

IMPURE WATER IN

PUMP
20 psi

FILTER

HIGH PRESSURE PUMP
1500 psi

IMPURITIES OUT

PURIFICATION UNIT

MEMBRANE

PURIFIED WATER

PRODUCT WATER

But it now seems promising that we can look forward to tremendous strides in this system of water purification. Gulf Oil, Culligan and Eastman Kodak are sponsoring vast research in this area. *High purity water*—between 90 and 97 percent of the dissolved mineral (and organic) solutions, and over 99 percent of the suspended and colloidal particles are rejected by the special membrane which has been developed for this process by these companies in their research. The product water from this new research is ultra-clear, low in dissolved solids, practically free from hardness components and essentially sterile as produced. This makes a close second to distilled water.

9. DE-IONIZED WATER. A process of exchanging "hard" ions for "soft" ions. The total ions are still present. The end result is the same. But the water has the appearance of being distilled. (Nature recognizes transformation but not extinction!) Since water leaving the sodium-cation exchanger has little hardness, it contains sodium salts.

10. DISTILLED WATER. This is water which has first been turned into steam so that all of its impurities are left behind. Then through condensation, it is turned back into pure water. It is the *only* pure water, the only water free from all contamination. Distilled water may well be considered the only pure water on earth.

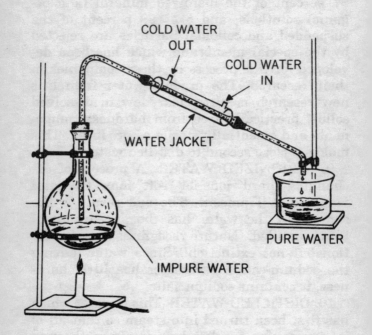

COLD WATER OUT

COLD WATER IN

WATER JACKET

PURE WATER

IMPURE WATER

**SIMPLE DISTILLATION PROCESS**

**Bottled water**

Bottled water has recently become a popular source of supposedly "pure" water. However, only a handful of states have regulations concerning bottled water. The Food and Drug Administration (FDA) has some guidelines and controls over water sold between the states. But it has no authority over bottled water that has been made or sold within state lines. Descriptions of bottled water may also be vague and easily misunderstood. The statement "bottled water" does not guarantee purity. The FDA should establish uniform standards of quality and a routine program of surveillance of the bottled water industries. It is considering the creation of formalities necessary to establish bacteriological, chemical and radioactive standards for bottled water.

In some cases, tap water (it costs about 1 cent for 22 gallons) is passed through a cellulose filter and then sold in bottles at a markup of 70 cents a gallon—more than 1600 times the cost of the water from your tap, and purified very little. So if you are buying bottled water, be sure of your source.

*The New York Daily News* revealed that, "One sampling of a popular brand turned up about 15,000 colonies of noncoliform bacteria in a single quart of water. City tap water averages 0 to 3 such colonies per quart. This bacteria is not necessarily harmful, but it does indicate that the water might be conducive to the growth of harmful bacteria."

According to tests conducted by the city's own water-testing laboratory, about seven samples of four popular brands of bottled water contained assorted bacteria averaging from 1,000 to 15,000 colonies per quart. While there is question over whether or not this amount of noncoliform bacteria can be harmful, there is no doubt that bottled water is not always as "pure" as suggested.

There are six main types of labeling on bottled water. They include:

1. *Electrified water*. When an electric current is passed through the solution of an electrolyte, the positively charged portions are attracted by and migrate toward the positive electrode. Electrolytes are called *ions* from the Greek verb meaning "to move." This electrodialysis process does *not* remove the viruses and bacteria.

2. *De-mineralized water*. This is water passed through a resin filter. It removes most of the minerals but, again, no filter is fine enough to filter out deadly viruses and bacteria. As the filter clogs, the dead bacteria form a breeding ground for more bacteria. Also, the chemical in the resin enters the water.

3. *Spring water*. There are very few good springs near large bottling companies. This means that many companies demineralize and "reconstitute" any available tap water, bottle it and offer it under a trade name with the illusion that it is "natural spring water."

Authentic spring water may be of any de-

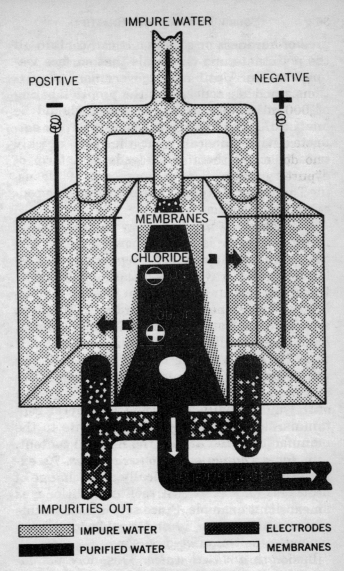

AN ELECTRODIALYSIS CELL

gree of hardness or softness. It can contain all
the pollutants and chemicals that surface waters contain. Until more government regulations are made concerning the proper labeling
of bottled water, all spring water should be
analyzed. Many springs are so excessively saturated with minerals that the body quickly
tries to expel them. This leads to a form of
dysentery which offers an impression of "cleans-
ing," but which can be unhealthy, causing constipation or colitis.

4. *Mountain water*. This may be deceptive. If
mountain water is fed by snow or glaciers, it
can be comparatively soft, depending on how
far the water travels down the mountainside.
However, mountain water can pick up air pollutants and some ground hardness. To check
any kind of water for its mineral contents,
have several gallons run through a distiller. If
there is residue on the bottom of the still, the
water contains inorganic minerals. Regardless
of which kind of bottled water you buy, the
only way to really know which mineral contaminants are in the water is to write to the
manufacturer and ask for the mineral content.

5. *Ion-exchange or de-ionized water*. As explained before, this is basically an exchange of
hard ions for soft ions. A zeolite conditioner is
an excellent example. Since salt is used in this
system, such water is undesirable for hyper-
tensive or salt-restricted persons.

6. *Steam distilled water*. This may not always be distilled. It may be "electrified," "de-

ionized," "filtered," "de-mineralized" or even tap water.

The best way to prove to yourself that it is actually distilled water is to home-distill it yourself. The residue left on the bottom of the distiller receptacle will prove to you whether the water is actually distilled or not.

If you do buy distilled water in bottles, consider your source. Many large steam distilleries use huge boilers to generate steam. The steam is then sent through long coils of copper tubing to convert the steam to water. Enroute, the distilled water picks up copper and other inorganic minerals. A home distiller has a very short route from the boiler to the condensing container. This is most important.

Sometimes, distilled water lies in large vats before bottling. This allows bacteria to enter the vat. Also, commercially produced distilled water can become contaminated if exposed to air. (It should be bottled immediately after distilling for purity.) Also, bacteria can multiply if bottled water is not refrigerated, and this is not always done with commercial distilled water. There are many arguments for the home distiller as a source of good, pure water.

In *Physician and Sportsmedicine* (18/1:49, 1990), it was pointed out that bottled water, while seemingly tasting better, may be more contaminated with bacteria than other water because a lack of chlorine permits bacteria to multiply when stored at room temperature for several days. Cyclists and other athletes who carry non-chlorinated water in unsterilized plastic bottles are especially at high risk. The magazine recommended as an alternative that one can distill water, a day's supply at a time, using a home water distiller.

Municipal tap water in many large cities is so heavily chlorinated that it is undrinkable. Many Americans are turning to bottled drinking water. But as we have said, there is no assurance that bottled water is either what it says it is or pure. You pay much, much more for bottled water than tap water. There may be no intrinsic difference at all.

Steam-distilled water is safe, since the process removes inorganic minerals, chemicals, viruses and bacteria, but make sure that you know the reputation of the distiller. There are good water distiller companies and dedicated men who supply this water, so take time to search for a reliable firm. But making your own distilled water is the most certain, economical, convenient way to have your personal supply of virgin, pure water always at hand.

## REFLECTIONS

*From the beginning, man settled at fresh water sources. Today, the beautiful hamlet situated at the side of a stream is regarded merely as being picturesque. In early days, however, the stream was essential to the life of the community.*

\* \*

*Land without water is land without life. The moon is sterile, barren, dead and waterless. If its seas were filled with water how different its relationship to the earth would be.*

# CHAPTER 3

# Water—Liquid Lifeline of Health

Because water is abundant and cheap, we take it for granted. But our lives depend upon it. We are creatures of water. The human body is almost three-fourths water. We drink five times our weight of water every year. This is a world of water. This liquid lifeline of health covers three-fourths of the earth's surface, on which there are 328 million cubic miles of water.

Over 350 billion gallons of water are used every day in the United States. All but a fraction of this amount is returned to streams, lakes and the ground and is available for future reuse. More than 90 percent of this 350 billion gallons of water is used by agriculture and industry, most of it supplied by them. Public supplies, serving domestic, commercial, public and industrial needs, amount to 25 billion gallons a day. This is about 150 gallons each day for every man, woman and child served by public systems.

On the average, each individual American uses 60 gallons of water daily in his home for drinking, cooking, laundering, household cleaning, bathing, shaving, lawn sprinkling, car washing and backyard swimming pools.

Commercial uses account for more than 20 gallons of the daily per capita use. We benefit directly from these uses. This water may be used for cooling systems in stores where we shop and offices where we work; it's the water in our dentist's office, restaurants, beauty salon and barber shop. Industry provides huge quantities of water for itself. It also uses water from the public system equivalent to 50 gallons per day for each person in a community. That water, too, benefits us directly, providing us with goods and jobs.

Another 10 gallons of the 150 gallons utilized daily for each community resident goes for public needs—water for sprinkling streets, municipal swimming pools, public drinking fountains, parks, public buildings and fire-fighting. The remaining 10 gallons per capita per day that the water utility must process and deliver in the community is, unfortunately, lost. Leaks and breaks in pipe-lines are inevitable, but improved methods of monitoring help keep these losses to a minimum.

*Water and your health*

Writing in *Food,* Yearbook of the U.S. Department of Agriculture, 1959, Dr. Olaf Mickelsen of the National Institute of Health, tells us:

"Next to oxygen, water is the most important factor for survival of man and animals. A person can do without food for five weeks or more, but without water he can survive for only a few days. The longer an individual goes without water, the greater the number and severity of symptoms he shows."

"Weakness, lassitude, thirst and dryness of the mouth are the first signs of dehydration. Loss of weight and mental confusion set in later. The individual becomes uncooperative and sullen. The cheeks become pale and the lips are dry and bluish. The skin loses its elasticity. The eyeballs have a sunken appearance. The volume of urine decreases, and its specific gravity rises. At the end, the respiration ceases, even though the pulse and general circulation may be well maintained. The volume of blood is maintained at the expense of the water within the body cells. The central nervous system undergoes the same dehydration as the cells in the remainder of the body and is the first area to show functional changes."

Our bodies lose water by various means. The kidneys are the most important, reflecting our drinking habits and varying with the individual. We also lose water through the air we breathe—we can talk and walk away a third of a quart of water a day this way. High altitude increases loss of water by the same means. Dr. Mickelsen has found that "The lower concentrations of oxygen in the air at elevations above 8,000 feet produce a compensatory increase in both the rate and depth of breathing. Furthermore, the absolute amount of moisture in the air at high altitudes is low. Since the expired air is practically saturated with moisture, the amount of water removed from the respiratory passages at high altitude is greater."

Through our skin we lose water in two different ways. One of them is "insensible" (or imperceptible) perspiration; this can amount to half a quart a day. The other is through sweat, of which we are well aware. Sweat differs from insensible perspiration in that it contains sodium chloride, urea and trace amounts of calcium, potassium and some of the water-soluble vitamins.

"The water lost in sweat," says Professor Mickelsen "should be replaced as soon as possible to forestall fatigue, which is one of the earliest symptoms shown by individuals who are short of water. To maintain your work efficiency during hot weather, you must consume water through the period of exposure to heat."

Hormones are vitally involved in the use of water in our metabolic processes, says Dr. Mickelsen. "One of them is vasopressin, which is produced by the posterior pituitary. A deficiency of it produces diabetes insipidus, a condition characterized by grave thirst and large amounts of urine. Treatment with vasopressin reduces the urine volume to normal.

"Another group of hormones, produced by the adrenal cortex, influences water in the body through their action on sodium and potassium metabolism. The inter-relationship of water and salt metabolism is so close that a change in the amount of sodium in the body is practically always accompanied by a corresponding change in the amount of water."

Dr. Mickelsen emphasizes the value of water. He says *It is well to remember that it is more important to have an adequate intake of water than it is to have enough calories.*

"Water for drinking should be free of unpleasant odors and flavors in order to make sure that the individual will ingest enough to meet his requirements."

### How water acts as the "lubrication" of your body

*Rose's Foundations of Nutrition* (5th edition, pps. 118-120) explains that water is an essential constituent of living protoplasm. No cell functions when it is absolutely dry, and most cells must be constantly bathed in fluid in order to do their work.

Furthermore, human cells depend on having their food transported to them over a fluid route—the blood—a demand which alone requires about ten pounds of water to be in circulation constantly. Waste-bearing water (urine) is necessary to flush away the end products of metabolism. And without water to moisten the surface of the lungs there can be no intake of oxygen or expulsion of carbon dioxide.

Dr. W. B. Cannon, the famous physiologist-author of *Wisdom of the Body,* explains it in a nutshell: "Water is the vehicle for food materials absorbed from the digestive canal; it is the medium in which chemical changes take place that underlie most of our obvious activities; it is essential in the regulation of body temperature and it plays an important part in mechanical services such as lubrication of joint surfaces."

### Water in your digestive process

Without sufficient water, food cannot be properly digested, absorbed and carried to all parts of the body through the bloodstream. In fact, the entire complex process of digestion consists of hydrolysis—the reaction of food constituents with water—in which the biological reaction of water with proteins, starches, sugars and fats produces substances which the body cells can use in their own functions.

In the stomach, water stimulates the gastric glands to hasten digestion. In the intestine, the dilution of solid food by liberal intake of water facilitates absorption of nutrients and the excretion of waste.

The very first step in the digestive process occurs in the mouth where saliva (99-½ percent water) starts the breakdown of carbohydrates.

In the stomach, meat and other proteins are digested by the gastric juices, which are 90 percent water. From here, the food, now in a comparatively fluid state, enters the upper section of the small intestine, known as the duodenum. There the enzymatic secretions of the duodenal wall itself, as well as the liver and pancreas (90 percent water) complete the digestive process. The food then passes through other sections of the small intestine, into the large intestine or colon, and from there into the rectum.

Water is absorbed into the body throughout the digestive process, though much less absorption takes place in the upper portion of the digestive system than in the lower. Little nutriment is absorbed from the stomach.

It has been estimated that three and one-half to five and one-half quarts of water are used by the body daily in the digestive process—about a quart and one-half of saliva, one or two quarts in the gastric juices, and the same amount in bile and other secretions. A substantial portion of this is reabsorbed through the intestinal wall to be used in carrying nutritive substances through the body.

*Water in your waste elimination*

Water is also essential to the excretion of soluble wastes through lungs, skin and kidneys. The walls of the tiny air sacs that comprise the lungs must be moistened continuously so that oxygen can enter the body and carbon dioxide be expelled. Not only the lungs, but the nose, throat, trachea and bronchial branches of the respiratory tract are coated with fluid. Unless the atmosphere is heavily laden with moisture, about a pint of liquid a day is lost through exhalation. To replace such losses, a steam vaporizer or humidifier which restores moisture to dry air, is often prescribed by physicians to provide relief for certain respiratory complaints.

Under normal conditions of temperature and activity, the kidneys are the principal avenue of water elimination. The amount varies with the amount of water intake. As a general rule, a quart of water passing through the kidneys will carry with it one and one-half ounces of soluble waste. In a normal adult, the amount of urine varies with fluid intake; it can also be reduced by an increase in the amount of water lost through sweating without compensating intake. However, there is a lower limit of one-third of a quart below which the amount of urine never falls. As long as there is any metabolic activity at all, no matter how reduced its rate, wastes are produced which must be excreted through the kidneys.

We must think of water in circulation as one of the conditions of health. Whatever its source, it is carried about and does its work without being chemically altered, leaving the body as water, by way of kidneys, lungs, skin and bowels.

## Water and your circulation

About 90 percent of blood plasma is water. This liquidity allows blood plasma to circulate freely throughout the body carrying vital substances with it. Among these substances are food, gases, inorganic salts, waste products, protective substances and those which promote growth and action.

All these materials contribute in some way to maintaining the necessary balance between blood cells and surrounding tissue. The plasma at one time or another contains every product which tissue cells obtain from the outside and use, and all substances produced by cells which are transported to other organs to be used by them or excreted from the body.

In spite of the fact that materials are added and removed at many points, plasma tends to maintain a constant composition. Entering the blood, for example, are oxygen at the lungs, absorbed water and food from the intestines, hormones from the glands of internal secretion, metabolic wastes of many kinds from all cells, and foods such as glucose from storage depots. Leaving the blood are nutriments for all cells, excess foods into storage regions, oxygen into tissues, water and other substances into secretory organs such as the liver; kidneys, sweat glands and digestive glands and carbon dioxide into the lungs.

### Water and temperature regulation

One of water's most distinctive properties is its ability to absorb heat readily. This is extremely important to living organisms which must maintain a constant internal temperature in the face of marked external variations. For optimum functioning, the human body must maintain an internal temperature of 98.6°F. under conditions which may vary from the summer desert to the winter Arctic. The water lost in perspiration should be replaced as soon as possible to forestall fatigue—one of the earliest symtoms of water shortage. To maintain your efficiency during hot weather, you must be careful to replenish your fluid supply throughout the period of exposure to heat.

### Water protects your body

Water lubricates your joints and acts as a cushion to protect the body from injuries resulting from impact and shock. It makes it possible for organs that rub together to slide smoothly. It also serves to maintain pressure in various parts of the body, such as the eyeballs. The muscles, which are 75 percent water, must have water to contract and maintain proper tonus. Good muscle tone itself serves to protect your body.

*How much water do you need?*

Generally speaking, a daily liquid allowance is often set at about ten or eleven glasses. About two pints of this is supplied by solid food. The remaining five or six glasses must come from liquids.

The simplest way to take care of this vital necessity is to develop early a drinking pattern that becomes as automatic as brushing the teeth. A sensible schedule might be one glass of liquid in the morning, two or three more between meals and one before going to bed.

Water is nature's own liquid lifeline of health. But today, with problems of pollution, with poisonous additives coming from tap water as well as the presence of inorganic minerals, our drinking water may be anything but desirable. Let us see what is happening to it and how it can be improved to provide us with a steady source of pure water.

## CONSIDER OUR TREASURE

*Water is a unique substance. Because it is cheap, we take it for granted. Because it is scarce and priceless, we shouldn't.*

# CHAPTER 4

# The Pros and Cons of Pure Water

Since the startling discovery of widespread pollutants in our drinking water has been splashed in screaming headlines in our newspapers and magazines, and also reported constantly on the radio and television, there has been much controversy about alternatives. Here are some of the arguments:

*Distilled water*. A water distiller removes such contaminating dangers as fluorides, chlorine and impurities from the air, earth and plumbing. It also removes those unassimilable inorganic minerals which are considered unhealthy to body accommodation. There are two kinds of minerals: organic and inorganic. Your body receives inorganic minerals from the water you drink. It receives organic minerals from the food you eat, which is why a balanced diet including raw fresh fruits and vegetables should

be eaten daily. Distilled water serves a two-
fold purpose: it prevents inorganic minerals
from entering your system and removes inorganic mineral deposits already there. Organic
minerals are absorbed and remain in your
tissues.

*Rain water.* Rain water is considered "God's
water" or "living water" in Burma, which has
an average yearly rainfall of 200 inches. The
people of Burma drink only rain water and
reportedly have the lowest incidence of heart
attacks and cancer. They get their organic minerals from fruits, vegetables and whole grains.
However, our rain water meets too many pollutants as it falls from the atmosphere to be in
any way considered equal in purity with that
in Burma.

*"Hard" vs. "soft" water.* Arguments rage about
these two, and remain inconclusive. Softened
water, often called "conditioned" water, is saturated with sodium (salt) which has been proven
to cause heart attacks. Distilled water has NO
sodium in it. Soft water can carry many harmful trace minerals and still be soft. Artificial
water softeners, when installed by a reputable
company, carry a warning not to use the softened water for drinking purposes. It is perfectly fine for bathing and laundry.

Many doctors have researched the harmful
effects of both hard and soft water. It was reported in *Prevention* magazine that a team of
doctors with the Welsh National School of Medicine sought to find out the reason for occur-

rences of central nervous system malformations, including anencephaly and spina bifida. (A spinal defect in which the spinal cord does not close completely and the membranes surrounding the spinal cord, the meninges, are ruptured.) Drs. C. R. Lowe, C. J. Roberts and S. Lloyd found that the drinking of hard water had a favorable influence. They concluded that "There is an obvious tendency for malformation rates to decrease as the hardness of the related water supplies increases" after examining 92,982 infants and ascertaining that 743 had defects in their neural tubes, a region consisting of the brain and spinal cord.

Drs. Anderson, LaRichie and Mackay reported in the *New England Journal of Medicine* conducting experiments to find out whether sudden heart attacks were greater in soft water areas than in hard water areas. The results pointed to soft water as a contributor to greater heart attacks. (Other researchers believe that soft water has inorganic elements which may not add to the hardness but may still lead to heart attacks.) The three doctors offered an inconclusive summary:

"It is also possible that our present findings are entirely fortuitous, and that the differences that we found . . . are unrelated to 'water hardness,' but are the result of other factors such as climate, population density and socioeconomic levels. Although it is now well established that mortality from ischemic heart disease may be related to water hardness, the mechanism remains obscure."

On the other hand, many believe that the harder the water, the greater the susceptibility to heart distress. Dr. Henry A. Schroeder, a well-known trace mineral expert at Dartmouth Medical School, made observations from a U.S. geological survey of water supplies made in 1,315 cities covering 90 percent of the urban and 58 percent of the total population. He found that in states where the water is above-average in hardness there is an increase in problems of heart-artery trouble as well as serious heart attacks.

Further tests conducted in many American, British, Swedish and Japanese cities reached the same conclusion: the harder the water, the greater the risk of heart trouble. Some believe that arterial stenosis (narrowing of the arteries) may be more prevalent in areas of the country where there is hard water.

But Dr. Schroeder also felt that the blame is not entirely to be placed upon soft or hard water, but upon various pollutants and wastes that the water picks up from the soil and water mains. We see that this is a problem since copper, lead, iron and galvanized water mains are sources of contamination that can poison our water.

However, the main culprit, according to Dr. Schroeder, is cadmium. This is a tin-white, malleable, ductile, bivalent, metallic element used especially in protective platings and in bearing metals. Galvanized mains (used particularly in Canada and Wales) contain trace amounts of this deadly contaminant, easily picked up by soft water. Cadmium is a competitor with zinc in coenzyme processes. This metal replaces zinc in metabolic activities related to fat utilization. It is Dr. Schroeder's belief that cadmium is the guilty element in the pathogenesis of both arteriosclerosis and hypertension.

Water nitrates are another source of reported danger. This chemical is linked to the sudden death of infants. As reported in *Life* magazine (January 30, 1970, p. 87), "In the San Joaquin Valley of California, agricultural fertilizers high in nitrogen have found their way into drinking water supplies to the extent that it has caused the death of small infants by cutting down the ability of their red blood cells to carry oxygen. Pediatricians are warning mothers not to give their babies tap water or softened water."

At the American Heart Association meeting in October, 1963, Dr. Denham Harman of the University of Nebraska School of Medicine, stated that ". . . the extra copper in soft water caused a higher number of fatal heart attacks than where people drank hard water." The doctor explained that copper serves as a catalyst in the rapid burning of fats in the blood. Byproducts of an excessive degree of oxidation act as irritants on blood vessel walls, thereby promoting the formation of fatty deposits. This burning or oxidation also depletes much needed oxygen for the tissues. (This is another point in favor of drinking distilled water.)

*Soft water risks.* In addition to a slow artery-choking action, soft water is considered more corrosive to metal pipes than hard water. Soft water pours out with an excess of impurities. As it travels along copper, lead and galvanized mains, soft water picks up deadly minerals, and still rates as soft water.

In many reported situations, lead poisoning has resulted from the erosion of lead by soft water running through lead pipes and delivering the metal right from the water tap.

This may be a reason why soft-water areas often show a higher rate of malformations of the central nervous system. Lead poisoning is directly responsible for brain damage. Furthermore, an expectant mother who drinks soft water containing even smaller amounts of lead in it might transfer enough of this lethal metal to her unborn child to retard growth of its brain and spinal cord.

Softened water also appears to inhibit the growth of plants and flowers. This attests to the low mineral and high sodium content of soft water.

If water comes into contact with sodium, it will absorb it whether it be softer or harder. Rain water, which is distilled, has no sodium, and the plants flourish. The suggestion is not to put a blanket condemnation on the water, but instead condemn the salt in the water. The salt can be removed by distillation. Water, itself, is healthful. *Rather, the inorganic ingredients in water are unhealthful and should be removed through distillation.*

Your clothing and dishes may not get clean in hard water. The answer is simple: use a water softener only in your hot water. Reserve your cold distilled water for all cooking and drinking.

Many scientists believe that old age and death (unless by accident) is traced to the accumulation of water poisons within the body. The famous Dr. Alexis Carrel made heart tissues "immortal" by regularly washing away the age-causing wastes of the cells.

Pure water appears to be a wonderful solvent to nourish the body and wash away the body's pollutions.

### *How to test the hardness of your water*

Here is an easy test you can perform right in your kitchen sink. Fill a small bottle to the one ounce level (two tablespoons) with tap water. Now, using an eyedropper, add tincture of green soap (available at any local pharmacy), one drop at a time, shaking the bottle vigorously after each drop. The point at which the mixture foams indicates the degree of hardness or softness of the water. If it foams after one or two drops, the water is soft; from 3 to 6 drops, the hardness increases to medium.

Water for domestic use should contain less than nine drops or "grains" as the measurement for water hardness is called. A level of six grains is considered satisfactory.

It is a simple test but it may very well save your health and improve your life.

If you are given any commercial ratings about your water, be aware of this: "soft water" is soft only when compared to water which is harder. "Softened water" is hard water run through a water softener. Hard ions are exchanged for soft ions, but the total is still there. Softened water is related directly to irregular heart pulse beats and heart attacks.

### Mineral waters vs. pure waters

It is believed that mineral waters help furnish mineral elements for body metabolism. But there is scientific proof to suggest that many of these minerals are in an inorganic (dead) form. While they may enter the circulation, they cannot be used in the physiological process of building the human cell. These inorganic minerals only interfere with the delicate and complex biology of the body. They may also overwork the kidneys.

For example, it would be biologically impossible to nourish the body with iron by taking "iron filings" or any other form of inorganic iron. The best way to nourish the body with iron is through fresh and, preferably, raw fruits and vegetables.

With this in mind, we can see that mineral water may be giving "dead" or "inorganic" minerals to the body which cannot be properly assimilated.

Water purified through distillation is free from inorganic calcium-magnesium compounds. The deposits of these inorganic substances in the system contribute to hardening of the arteries and tissues or the "aging syndrome." Exploratory research is revealing that the aging process is often traced to the hardness in our drinking water. To this, we must also include the chlorines and fluorides.

**Life + Health = Pure Water**

Scientific research continues on the life and health-giving qualities of pure water. Every student of physics conducts experiments with distilled water. Kidney machines use only distilled water.

Nature designed water to attract minerals until it reaches a saturation point. This saturation point could go beyond 35,000 PPM (sea water). Water is further regarded as the greatest solvent known to mankind. Its purpose is to pick up inorganic minerals as it flows over the ground. The longer it flows or sinks into the ground, the harder it becomes.

Because plants require inorganic minerals, water becomes the chief carrier of these minerals to the roots of these plants. But hard water can have an adverse effect on plants. For example, mineral deposits can *seal* the pores of plants just as they can put a sealed film around cells in your body. If it rained hard water, that water would have a deleterious effect on plants. If plants cannot take in enough carbon dioxide and eliminate oxygen, the plants die of asphyxia. In humans, however, the reaction is in reverse, since humans breathe *in* oxygen and *exhale* carbon dioxide.

Farmers and horticulturists agree that rain water is much better "food" for plants. A spring rain will green a lawn overnight. Rain water, as a solvent, attracts the inorganic mineral deposits in the pores of plants and allows for freer circulation of carbon dioxide and oxygen.

Here is a case in point. My father was a thresher man for 40 years. He assigned a job to me, to haul water for his steam engine. Every Sunday we would begin by cooling the boiler, then we would climb inside and hammer away the scales that formed on the inside.

We discovered that the *harder the water, the more scales formed on the boiler*.

Conversely, the less hard the water, the *fewer* the scales formed.

We soon learned that water from the creek was less hard or lower in organic calcium and magnesium, than the water from the farmer's well, because it formed fewer scales on the boiler.

The fact is that pure distilled water (or any water) will dissolve nails. This is a law of nature. But the point is, which one of the two waters would you prefer to drink? Can our bodies utilize the molecules found in iron? Or could these molecules be a possible cause of many of our aging diseases? Speaking simply, we realize that the chemical formula of water is $H_2O$ and regardless of what else it contains, any other substance found in it is added to it.

When perspiration from the human body evaporates into the air, it is later condensed into liquid. That water is pure distilled water of an organic variety because it came from a living organism—the human body.

So it is the same with the liquid from any other kind of living organism.

Distillation was mentioned by Aristotle as far back as the fourth century B.C. as a method for using sea water. As we have said before, nature uses it when the water from the earth is drawn into the air to condense and fall as rain. The water distilled by man goes through a process of boiling until steam forms; rapidly cooling the steam and collecting the pure drops that result as it condenses eliminates all impurities and prepares the water for optimum use by the body.

## OUR GREATEST GIFT

*Water is nature's greatest gift to all growing things. There is vitality contained in fresh distilled water that is as mysterious as life itself—some mysterious force that may not yet be fully understood.*

# CHAPTER 5

# Water Hardness and Your Health

Water hardness results when calcium and magnesium within the soil dissolve. Both minerals are present in almost all natural, untreated water in varying concentrations. Symptoms of hardness include whitish scale deposits on your plumbing and appliances; soap deposits on laundry, dishes and the bathtub; less-than-satisfactory cleaning action from soaps and detergents; and less efficiency from your water heater. While not imperative, some water softener may be desirable.

The most common household water softening system (ion exchange) uses a resin bed to exchange the hardness mineral ion (calcium and magnesium) for the soft ions of sodium. The harder the water, the more sodium the system adds to it. For each grain per gallon of hardness, 7.5 milligrams of sodium are added per quart of water.

If you're on a restricted sodium diet, consult your physician about drinking softened water. One option is to install the treatment system so that it bypasses the cold water at the kitchen sink. A potassium ion exchange system is a more costly alternative to a sodium ion exchange unit, but there is no associated health risk. A reverse osmosis unit can be installed to reduce hardness. Use untreated water for watering plants, lawns and gardens.

Ion exchange systems can also remove low quantities of iron and manganese. However, if these minerals are present in high concentrations, the system could suffer from a shortened resin bed life and unnecessary repeated backwash cycles. If iron and manganese are also causing water quality problems, these minerals will need to be removed before softening.

### Is your tap water "off"?

Many people have stopped drinking tap water because they are concerned that water sources are endangered by chemicals accidentally or unknowingly released into the environment. Anxiety continues to grow about groundwater contamination from landfills, illegal dumping of hazardous and toxic wastes, highway de-icing salts, salt-water encroachment and leaking underground storage tanks.

Spring water seeps or "springs" to the earth's surface from underground aquifers. If the bottle label does not state "natural," the water may have undergone some processing—the addition of minerals, for example.

Artesian well water comes from a confined underground aquifer. Underground pressure forces the water to the surface in pipes drilled through the upper layer of rock.

*Distilled water* is processed by heating and condensing the vapor. This product is free of most mineral salts.

*Still water* is noncarbonated; it can be spring, well or municipal tap water.

*Sparkling water* is carbonated, as a rule, by the injection of carbon dioxide gas.

*Naturally carbonated* means that the water is effervescent in its underground source. Club soda, seltzer and other sparkling mineral waters are carbonated by manufactured carbon dioxide.

*Club soda,* typically, is tap water that has been filtered and carbonated and to which minerals and mineral salts have been added.

*Seltzer* is usually tap water that is merely filtered and carbonated. Some brands claim to be "salt free," meaning that they contain no sodium ions.

*Purified water* is water produced by distillation, deionization, reverse osmosis or other methods.

*Natural water* is bottled or vended spring, artesian well or well water unmodified by mineral addition or deletion. However, natural water may be filtered and treated.

*Soft water* is water with a low mineral salt content.

*Hard Water* is water with a high mineral salt content.

### Is your water "good"?

What constitutes "good" water is controversial in many circles. The EPA has selected more than 30 possible contaminants that it believes should not be in water. In 1990, 30 more contaminants were added to the list. Yet not everyone agrees with what the EPA allows in water. Some people feel that fluoride, which is said to help protect children's teeth from cavities, should not be in water. Others believe that the EPA allows too much chlorine to disinfect water. Yet, according to the EPA, a byproduct of chlorine, trihalomethane (TTHM) may be of more concern as a possible contaminant than chlorine. With the use of home treatment systems and bottled water, you can minimize any potential risks to your health.

### Choosing a water treatment system

You need to choose the system that eliminates the specific contaminants found in your water. Also look at maintenance and cost factors. Some systems require regular filter changes. If you forget to change a filter, your water will become even more contaminated than without the system.

Also, how often must the system be replaced? Some systems cost a lot but last a long time.

And do not be misled by a system that states it is EPA approved. This means the working parts will not contaminate water; it does not mean that the actual filtering system has been approved or promoted by the EPA.

You have your options of the following basic systems:

1 *Activated alumina*—reduces arsenic and fluoride.

2. *Activated carbon filters*—reduces mercury (both organic and inorganic, trichloroethylene (TCE), and trihalomethanes (TTHM).

3. *Aeration*—reduces TCE.

4. *Disinfection*—reduces coliform bacteria.

5. *Distillation*—reduces arsenic, barium, fluoride, lead, inorganic mercury, nitrate, TTHM, radium and coliform bacteria.

6. *Ion exchange (anion)*—reduces arsenic and nitrate.

7. *Ion exchange (cation) water softeners*—reduce barium, lead and radium.

8. *Reverse osmosis*—reduces arsenic, barium, fluoride, lead, inorganic mercury, nitrate, radium and coliform bacteria.

9. *Ultra violet radiation*—reduces bacteria and viruses in pre-filtered water.

There is a brighter side to the problem of drinking water. The revised Safe Drinking Water Act of 1986 mandates that water supplies be tested for many more pollutants than in the past; the general requirements for public water supplies are tightened. In a survey, it was found that tap water from San Francisco and

Los Angeles rated as high or better than many bottled waters in terms of taste and purity.

Florida and California have initiated their own tough water purity standards in addition to the federal guidelines. For example, Florida checks public water supplies for 130 chemicals every years. Other states are planning to implement tighter regulations as well to assure the quality of water sold in those states.

### Is country water any cleaner?

City dwellers seem to worry most about the safety and purity of their water. True that industrial pollution is an ever-growing threat in metropolitan areas; but on the other side of the coin, water purification techniques and standards are more rigid. It is believed that the larger the city, the better staffed it is in terms of qualified water purification engineers. Yet 20 percent of Americans are drinking water that is anything but clean or safe. And these people usually live in smaller water districts or else have to rely upon rural wells.

A major problem is the way in which pollutants infiltrate and penetrate through groundwater aquifiers. Any well will pick up pollutants from such sources as chemicalized farms, leaky underground gasoline tanks, abandoned mining sites, distant factories, old septic tanks and bacterial sources from a town garbage dump, even if it is located many miles away.

If you dig a deeper well, is that able to solve

the problem of water pollution. Not necessarily. Basically, surface soil does an inadequate job of filtering contaminants poured on the ground. Furthermore, even if the well is deeper, it is more likely to concentrate mineral contaminants such as arsenic and lead. Conversely, even if rural water sources are open to pollution, they seem to be less likely to be subjected to scientifically advanced purification techniques. Private sources of water such as rural wells are NOT subject to government testing as would be the rule with big city water supplies. Therefore, you can understand that country water is not cleaner than city water . . . it may be far worse!

### When good water becomes toxic

To determine if water is pure, you go to the source. But this is only part of the situation. In the old water system, lead pipes are able to contaminate water that was found to be good at the reservoir or city purification plant. If pipes are old and soft, lead is more readily withdrawn; this is found in many older houses as well as in any so-called antiquated water systems. If the water is more acidic, lead along with other undesirable minerals from pipes is more easily dissolved.

You may be able to reduce heavy metal contamination from your old pipes or from acidic water if you make this one rule: do not use water that has been sitting in your pipes for too long. If possible, run water for a few minutes before using it. And NEVER use hot tap water (it is a potent source of dissolved minerals) for consumption. Instead, start with cold water you then heat on your stove or in your microwave.

Do not overboil water that you suspect is saturated with heavy metals. Yes, boiling is important to overcome bacterial infestations in water but it will also cause a concentration of toxic metals.

### How can you tell if your water is bad?

Several warning signs should alert you to the possibility of toxic water, such as—

• Clear water that now looks murky or becomes suddenly cloudy. Chlorination causes some cloudiness but it will go away if the water is left to stand. Sediment-caused or bacteria-caused cloudiness will remain. Foaming water is a sign that could indicate bacterial contamination. Look for any floating particles of sediment.

• You can minimize or even destroy bacteria by boiling water at least 20 minutes. As for sediment, it can be settled out if you let your water remain standing in a glass container for a few hours.

• Sniff the water. Unusual smells could mean it is contaminated by chemicals.

• Taste the water. Any strange flavor could also be a sign of chemical contamination.

Finally, some home water purification systems can remove some contaminants but not all of them. If you do not change your water filters often enough, they are to be blamed for contributing to pollution by bacterial growth.

### *You cannot always detect water pollution*

Toxic hazards that penetrate your water do not all bring noticeable changes in smell, appearance and/or taste. For this reason, federal and local governments regularly monitor public water supplies. But if you own a private well or use water from such a source, it is not monitored and should receive testing on a regular basis.

If you use municipal water, ask the local water authority for the latest analysis of your tap water. If you use a private well, ask state regulatory boards or private companies in your vicinity about regular testing of your supplies.

### *Have you tested your tap water lately?*

Drinking water may contain any of nearly 1,000 contaminants, from benzene to lead to PCBs. In a 1987 study, the National Cancer Institute concluded that risk of developing bladder cancer rose with increased intake of beverages made with chlorinated surface water. And that describes the water supply for half of all U.S. households, according to the Nutrition Action Health Letter.

Surface water often contains decaying animal or plant material; when this water is treated with chlorine, cancer-causing compounds may form. Another problem with surface water and even ground water is that either can pick up lead on the trip from the purification plant to the tap.

The Centers for Disease Control estimates that 10.4 million children in the U.S. are exposed to significant amounts of lead in their drinking water. If your home has lead pipes or copper pipes with lead solder, and your water is acidic, you could be ingesting water with high lead levels. Testing water is the only sure way to know.

You should have your tap water tested if:

• You drink from your own well or other private water supply.
• You notice a change in your water's color, taste or odor.
• You suspect the presence of lead.
• You live near a hazardous waste dump, industrial park, chemical manufacturing plant or military base.

*Checking safety of your tap water*

How can you be sure your tap water is wholesome? According to a report in the *New York University Medical Center Health Letter,* here is a four-step plan to help make your water safer:

1. First thing in the morning, or whenever you first turn on the water after not using it for eight hours or more, let it run for several minutes to reduce lead levels in drinking or cooking water. Households with lead plumbing are most at risk; also questionable is lead used in the joint solder for copper plumbing.

2. Does your water taste bad or have a foul smell? It may have decayed material or infectious organisms. If you smell sulfur or petroleum, it may indicate contamination. If the water tastes strongly of chlorine, it would be best not to drink it. Report it to your local health department or your water supplier.

3. If your water is yellow, it is usually a sign of corroded pipes; brown discoloration may indicate underground pollution; green water may indicate algea. Be alert to any off colors to be reported to your health department or water supplier.

4. Cloudy water? Let it stand for a few moments to make sure it clears and nothing settles at the bottom. Those tiny bubbles make the water appear to be cloudy when first drawn from the tap, but they are harmless. If the water is still cloudy after standing, or if a sediment settles on the bottom, let the water run for a few minutes, then repeat this test. If it still remains cloudy or is sedimented, it is possible the water has solid particles of sand, mud or other material suspended in the water and should not be used. Report it immediately.

**Homemade water purification method**

The Environmental Defense Fund suggests this method of homemade water purification:

Put a coffee filter paper in a large funnel. Wash enough granular activated carbon (available from water treatment outlets and many large health food product sources) to fill one-quarter of the funnel.

To wash carbon, put it in a jar, fill it with water, cover and shake. Let the carbon settle and pour off the water at the top. Repeat until the water you pour off is clear.

Now set the funnel in a large clean jar. Add the carbon and slowly pour your tap water through the funnel.

Change the carbon every 21 days; or after 20 gallons of water have been filtered through it. Store the filtered water in your refrigerator.

**Pre-boiling your drinking water**

You will help purify your water if you boil it gently for 15 to 20 minutes; this helps evaporate many of the carcinogens. After boiling, bottle it and store it closed in your refrigerator.

If your water appears turbid (cloudy, indicating possible sewage contamination, it should be boiled for a minimum of ten minutes if you have no other source of water.

For an easier solution, of course, invest in a home water filter system, available from health food stores, by mail order, etc.

# WATER, WATER EVERYWHERE, BUT ...

*You may wonder how water becomes unfit to drink, even if it is so far from industrial areas. The reason is that insecticides, chemical fertilizers and herbicides are very concentrated in rural areas. Rain will wash off these chemicals, soaking them into the soil and into the groundwater that supplies water to the well. Even the overuse of natural manure fertilizers in a concentrated location will cause groundwater pollution with excessive nitrates.*

# CHAPTER 6

# How Good Water Can Help You Live Longer

Many people say that distilled water is dead water because a fish cannot live in it. Of course, a fish cannot live in any man-created water for any length of time. A fish needs the vegetation that grows in rivers, lakes and seas.

Pure water helps to dissolve the toxic poisons that accumulate in man's body. It helps to eliminate these toxic poisons through the kidneys; it passes through the kidneys without leaving inorganic pebbles and stones.

Every liquid prescription that is compounded in any drugstore the world over is prepared with distilled water. It is used in baby formulae and for many other purposes where absolutely pure water is essential.

Distilled water is purified rain water. If you wash your hair in distilled water, you will discover how soft it is. Just visualize how good it is for the rest of your body, inside and outside!

Water is a carrier of inorganic minerals and chemicals which were not designed to be accommodated by the body. Water, so designed, was *designed for plants!* Only after they have passed through the roots of plants do these inorganic minerals become organic (through photosynthesis) and capable of being assimilated into our tissues.

Distillation kills bacteria and viruses and removes complex chemicals, heavy dangerous inorganic substances, pesticides, chlorine and fluorides.

According to Rose's *Foundations of Nutrition,* "Since one kind of water takes most of the inorganic minerals into the body and leaves its mineral deposits there—and since another kind of water dissolves those mineral deposits and washes them out of the body, it is important to decide what kind of water to use in purifying the body—to change it from a stiffened and hardened old body to a body that is supple, buoyant and youthful with energy."

If you were to distill all the 6,500 gallons of water consumed during your lifetime, you could collect 420 glasses of solids. These solids settle in our tissue, joints, artery walls and short-cut nerve centers and seal every cell from the vital oxygen it needs.

When you lose weight during illness, your body functions decline. There is a loss of water, too. Mineral deposits become more concentrated. Your blood may become overly thick because of these deposits. Recovery from ill health may be slowed down or interfered with. To help protect against such problems, it is important to feed your body with pure water to make up for that which is lost during perspiration and feverish conditions.

Many have said that the chlorine in water could be boiled out. Many have suggested that even small amounts of chlorine could contribute to heart trouble. This means that if *small* amounts cause heart trouble, what will *large* amounts do? Boiling will remove chlorine if boiled long enough. But this is inconvenient. Who can boil water every day when traveling or pressed for time? What about all the other chemicals which do not boil out? This suggests that distilled water is the answer. On our polluted planet, 40 percent of our ocean life has disappeared. Arctic seals are dying. Fish are dying by the millions. This is the result of "dead" water. It is similar to much tap water. To compound the problem, we regularly hear about oil spills, such as the disastrous one on March 24, 1989, near Valdez, Alaska.

*Health Problems:* X rays show mineral deposits on the arteries, heart valves, joints, intestines and stones in the kidney and gallbladders. These are *inorganic* minerals, carried in by the water you drink. The average person who drinks water with the hardness of 26 grains, will drink many glasses of solids during an average life span. This is a lot of sludge.

But suppose he drinks water saturated with a hardness of 450 parts per million?

Think what happens to the inside of a tea kettle in one week. Realize what happens to the inside of your body in 30 years! How much calcium do you think will collect in your body by the time you are 30 years older? That is a clue to aging. The body grows stiffer and harder each year. Hard water, chlorinated, put through a kidney machine, can cause sudden death. It could also cause a *slow* death through daily use!

The U.S. Public Health Service, Department of Agriculture, Rural Electrification Administration stated about distilled water:

*"The only proven method of correcting cooking and drinking water pollution in the home is through the use of a home water distiller."*

## THE HYDROLOGIC CYCLE

*Water is never really consumed by man. It is merely used and reused. Most of the water that falls on land eventually is carried to the sea. There it evaporates and is drawn upward by the sun, where it forms clouds. It falls to earth as rain, snow, or sleet—and the cycle begins all over again. This is nature's way of purifying water. But alas, pollutants are combating purity.*

# CHAPTER 7

# How Pure Water Helps Improve Body Health

Pure, distilled water offers many methods of improving body health. For example:

The body, which is about three-fourths water, is able to hold all that water in the solid cellular structures because the lipids of which the body structures are constructed are insoluble in water under the conditions in which the body lives. Pure water offers this form of cellular regeneration.

The typical cell of an animal or plant consists of an outer permeable membrane and an inner semi-permeable membrane. Such elements as inorganic minerals cannot pass through the inner cell walls, and therefore cannot be used in the body's processes. Should they pass through the outer cell walls they can only be deposited in the space between the outer and inner walls, making it difficult for the needed organic minerals in the form of exogenous chemical compounds to pass through the fluids between the outer cell walls and the plasma membranes.

The *Encylopedia Britannica* explains that the plasma membrane, which encloses the cytoplasm (or inner structures of the cell composed of protoplasm) "is called the semipermeable membrane because it allows some molecules to pass but not others. Protein components such as amino acids pass more easily through the membrane than do many smaller molecules, so molecular size is not the crucial factor. A selective pumping action, according to the requirements of the cell, has been suggested."

T. H. Huxley, M.D. in his essay, "On the Physical Basis of Life," states that the inorganic minerals (as found in hard or soft water) *cannot* be used by any living body, animal, human or plant. He says that, "A solution of smelling salts in water, with an infinitesimal proportion of some other saline matters, contains all the elementary bodies which enter into the composition of protoplasm; but as I need hardly say, a hogshead of that fluid would not keep a hungry man from starving, nor would it save any animal whatever from a like fate."

The animal (and man is an animal) does not make protoplasm. Instead, it must receive it ready made from another animal or plant. Then it is metabolized by the body to sustain life.

The animal organism is able to metabolize this protoplasm into a form that can be used.

The eaten plant offers carbonic water acid, water and nitrogenous salts in a form of usable protoplasm.

No known plant can survive upon the uncompounded elements of protoplasm. If a plant is given carbon, hydrogen, oxygen, nitrogen, phosphorus, sulfur, it would still die, even if surrounded by all the needed elements of protoplasm.

But once the plant is given water, along with carbonic acid and the other needed elements, it has the necessary components in the proper form for survival.

The inorganic minerals and chemicals found in hard and soft water interfere with the metabolic processes. It is believed that those found in hard water are tucked into the joints, causing arthritis, constipation and hardening of the arteries. The unusable elements picked up by soft water are particularly dangerous to the heart, since they are closer to the uncompounded elements in protoplasm, but unassimilable in the form they enter the body.

Distilled water has no damaging effect on the heart. It takes nothing away from the heart by way of essential trace elements already incorporated into the structures of the heart. Nor does it deposit any unwanted material into the joints.

Water should be the purifier of the medium in which the body cells live and work. It serves a double purpose; it carries *in* nutritive elements and carries *out* waste. Most of our tap water holds in solution inorganic materials picked up from the ground in pipes or put in by man, such as chlorine or fluoride.

Inorganic minerals are food for the *soil*, but not for man. Rather than risk the assorted ills that water containing them may cause, the safe solution is to use distilled water. It takes one quart of water to eliminate 45 grams of wastes in the urine. To help the body in the vital function of the disposal of toxins and wastes, the most efficient medium should be used—and that is pure water.

## WATER IS UNIQUE

*Even today, water is not fully understood. It is the only substance that exists as a solid, a liquid, and a gas, in the earth's normal temperature range—often at the same time, and in the same place. While most substances contract when they solidify, water expands by 10 percent, becomes lighter than an equal volume of water, and floats. We call this ICE. Except for this amazing characteristic, lakes would freeze from bottom up, and life within would die.*

# CHAPTER 8

# Chlorine and Your Drinking Water

As a naturally occurring mineral in fruits, vegetables and raw juices, chlorine is vital to your health. Your body needs chlorine. It is often called "nature's broomstick" because it is able to wash out body wastes and help keep the bloodstream clean and sparkling. Chlorine is important. But chemicalized chlorine as created in a laboratory and NOT by nature is a partner with chemicalized chloride. Both are known as "wildcats" in the chemical field.

### Chemical chlorine

A medical dictionary says of chlorine that it is "a yellowish-green, gaseous element, of suffocating odor. It is a disinfectant, decolorant and an irritant poison. It is used for disinfecting, fumigating and bleaching, either in water purification or in medicine."

Chlorine is suffocating. It kills. If it is a disinfectant, it has an "odor" and an odor "suffocates." If it is put in our drinking water as a disinfectant, it again can "kill."

Chlorine is so potent it must be transported in rubberized tanks. Chlorine will eat its way through the toughest and thickest metals. Only with the greatest care and the most precise equipment, can it be but partially controlled. *Chlorine acts as swiftly as lightning.* One drop of chlorine added to a large vat of water will strike every water molecule at once. It is instantaneous!

Since water levels in our city tanks are never the same, the water entering the huge storage tanks varies. So does the chlorine content. Then individual water consumption, per person, varies. Some people will drink two glasses of water per day, others may drink ten glasses, and still carry the same body weight.

Under such circumstances, the heavy water drinker will consume ten times the chlorine. Take five times the poison of any kind, and note the rise in fatalities! This is serious. But it worsens when you realize that chlorine builds up in the body system. The man who takes in five times as much chlorine runs a greater risk of becoming poisoned.

In his book, *Coronaries—Cholesterol—Chlorine,* Joseph M. Price, M.D., describes a test of chlorine upon chickens. Two groups received the same diet. One group had chlorine added. When that group was later sacrificed and studied, every chicken had some circulatory and heart disease. The non-chlorine-taking chickens were in perfect health. Dr. Price tells us:

"The results were nothing short of spectacular! Within three weeks, there were grossly observable effects on both appearance and behavior. The experimental group became lethargic, huddling in corners, except at feeding time. Their features became frayed and dirty and the cockerels walked around with their wings hunched up, their feathers fluffed like they were always cold (the experiment was performed in an unheated barn in winter), their pale combs drooping. This appearance is most suggestive of symptoms resulting from clogging up of the micro-circulation.

"Meanwhile the control group was the epitome of vigorous health. They were much larger in size than the experimental group, active, quarrelsome, vigorous-appearing with smooth, clean, shiny features and bright combs held up erectly."

Some 95 percent of the chlorine-fed chickens died of heart conditions and circulatory diseases —but the chlorine-free group remained perfectly healthy.

If you live in a city with chlorinated water, remember that chlorine accumulates in your system. At times, the concentrations may be so great you can actually smell the chlorine. This should alert you to the need for a distillation machine in your own home.

We are living in a poisoned world. Vast majorities of illnesses can be traced to chemicals in our soil, air, water or through food processing and poison sprays. Little we eat or touch today has not been exposed to countless chemicals. They have a tendency to build up. There are so many new chemicals appearing in our foods today that governmental agencies cannot cope with them.

Many authorities trace the incidence of heart trouble not solely to cholesterol but to chlorine and poisons in our water supplies. Dr. Price believes strongly that chlorine contributes to atherosclerosis.

In a massive 700 page report, Ralph Nader's task force seriously indicted the quality of America's tap water. The report said, "Chemicals and viruses can and do pass through municipal purification systems to the household water user. These contaminants carry not only the risk of disease, but can cause cancer, birth defects and genetic damage."

## WHEN WAS WATER PURE?

*To live is to pollute. Man cannot avoid generating waste products. He cannot avoid altering water or changing its quality. But even before man came on the scene, water was being polluted. Nature was dirtying it, and on a grand scale. Water in nature has never been pure. Therefore distillation is so important. There is no purity, without distillation.*

# CHAPTER 9

# Fluorides and Drinking Water

At a press conference held March 20, 1990 in Washington, D. C., John Yiamouyiannis, Ph.D., called for a ban on public water fluoridation and demanded an investigation into a possible cover-up of the facts linking water fluoridation to cancer. Dr. Yiamouyiannis, who is president of the Safe Water Foundation, and a consultant for the Center for Health Action, Springfield, Mass., based his remarks on an analysis of the most recent federal animal study on fluoride and cancer. That study, which was conducted by the National Toxicology Program, a division of the United States Public Health Service, was ordered 13 years ago by the U.S. Congress. However, the official results of the study were not made public until January 1990.

Dr. Yiamouyiannis said that a number of different cancers and pre-cancerous cell growths were associated with fluoride intake in mice and rats, including hepatocholangiocarcinoma, a rare form of liver cancer, which turned up in both male and female mice drinking fluoridated water. Animals drinking non-fluoridated water did not develop the cancer. His analysis also confirmed the presence of a rare form of bone cancer, osteosarcoma, which was found in some of the rats and which was initially reported by the National Toxicology Program (NTP).

An additional analysis by Dr. Yiamouyiannis showed these changes in some of the rats: 1) Precancerous changes in oral squamous cells. These changes were also observed in animal studies conducted by Procter and Gamble in 1985; 2) An increase in squamous cell tumors and cancers; and 3) Thyroid follicular cell tumors as a result of increasing levels of fluoride in the drinking water.

"The NTP laboratory studies are not the first to show that fluoride leads to cancer," Dr. Yiamouyiannis said. "In 1988, researchers from Argonne National Laboratories, under contract by the United States Public Health Service, found that fluoride not only induces but promotes cancer. In a separate study, these Argonne researchers also confirmed the findings of scientists from the Nippon Dental University in Japan showing that the exposure of normal cells to fluoride transforms them into cancer cells. Any one of these studies would be sufficient to cause concern, and any two of them would be enough to suggest that fluoridation be discontinued. However, when you consider all of the studies, beginning in 1952 with Dr. A. Taylor at the University of Texas, Austin, to the present—over 50 anti-fluoridation studies—they create a public mandate to stop water fluoridation immediately."

Also present at the press conference to express their concern about fluoride were Susan Pare, president for the Center for Health Action; Dr. Robert Carton, president of the U. S. Environmental Protection Agency's union of scientists and professional workers; and Jacqueline Warren, representing the Natural Resources Defense Council.

"Based upon conclusive evidence that fluoride causes cancer in laboratory animals and coupled with the fact that recent federal and international studies show that water fluoridation does not reduce tooth decay, it's a mystery to us why water fluoridation is still being practiced and promoted," Susan Pare said. "Congress should act now to protect the public and stop fluoridation."

In an earlier statement as to why the public water supply should not be fluoridated, Dr. Jonathan Forman, chairman of the National Council to Evaluate Fluoridation, stated that:

"1. Fluorine is a mutant in both plants and animals. Exposure of seeds to fluorine produces all sorts of congenital defects in plants and grains from seeds thus exposed. (See H. F. Mc-

Donald, Ph.D. Fluoride Quarterly Report Vol. 2, No. 1, p. 5, 1969.)

"In the human, the use of fluoridated water in a like manner does damage to the chromosomes and produces Mongoloidism in the foetus. (Epidemiological studies by Rappaport; see his report on north central states in the U.S.A. before the French Academy of Medicine.)

"Other congenital defects no doubt will be found when looked for now that it has been established that fluorine does damage to chromosomes when it comes in contact with them.

"2. One of the finest Zoological Gardens is that of Philadelphia. It is noted for the health and nutritional state of its animals. But after the city water was fluoridated the animals began to die in great numbers from coronary disease, arteriosclerosis, myocardial fibrosis, and myocardial infarctions. Congressman Miller of Nebraska, a physician and former State Health Commissioner, found the same thing in Grand Rapids, Michigan after that city's water was fluoridated.

"3. Obesity is the most prevalent sign of malnutrition among our people. Obese persons, because of their high carbohydrate diet are predisposed to diabetes. The diabetic must drink several quarts of water each day and anyone who drinks more than three pints of fluoridated water daily has entered the poison zone—all admit this to be a fact. The incidence of diabetes is high in Ohio.

"4. Upon adequate exposure by contact, ingestion, or inhalation, humans become allergic to fluorine with manifestations of eczema, bronchitis and asthma.

"5. Fluoridation can cause goiter. Fluorine is a more active combiner than its sister halogen, iodine, and this can cause an iodine deficiency in the thyroid gland thus producing a goiter. Incidentally, the authorities in the city of Akron insisted on fluoridation even though this was the very place where it proved that iodine deficiency was the cause of goiter in the 'goiter belt.'

"6. It is well established that fluorides inhibit the enzymes having to do with nerve conduction but no studies have been made on the learning capacity or social behavior of persons whose nervous systems are being bathed in fluorides day in and day out, year in and year out. This should have been done before fluoridation was considered.

"7. Much is made by the proponents of fluoridation of the need of the poor who cannot or do not brush their teeth. This concern is commendable but, unfortunately, misdirected. Undernourished children are much more susceptible to the poisonous effects of fluorides than are well-nourished ones.

"8. Men and women who work in high temperatures and are given salt tablets to avoid the adverse effects of heat drink lots of water as does the diabetic patient and the individual with high blood pressure and hardened arteries in his kidneys. The latter must drink literally gallons of water to flush the toxic waste from his body since the kidneys can no longer handle it in the normal way. Anyone who drinks over three pints a day of fluoridated water is poisoning himself.

"9. The Canadian National Research Council has concerned itself with increased consumption of fluorides that has resulted from the use of fluoridated water in the processing of various foods and beverages. They concluded that an adult, drinking fluoridated water and using foods prepared with it (in the home and from the grocery), will be taking into his body a minimum of two milligrams of fluorine and it often will go as high as five. Our own Food and Drug Administration has repeatedly warned that the total intake of fluorine from all sources, especially during the time the teeth are forming, should not exceed two milligrams per day. Foods grown with heavy fertilization with phosphates (such as the commercial grower uses to produce volume) will contain fluorides. The amount will vary but some plants pick up more than others.

"10. Fluorides are sometimes present in industrial waste and, when they are, they are poisonous to fish if the concentration exceeds 1.5 parts per million (see Report of Committee On Water Control, April, 1960, U.S. Government Printing Office, p. 88. $3.00).

"11. There is such a demand for fluorides that a recent writer in *Chemical and Engineering News* predicts they will soon be hard to come by and costly. This already is coming true. The cost of fluoridation instead of being 10 cents per capita per year as stated by the proponents has already risen to $1.25 per capita per year. And even at that, several of the larger cities have had to reduce the level to 0.5 parts per million, whereas only a short time ago they were busy adjusting the level of fluorine in cities with a natural level of 0.5 ppm up to the 1 ppm they recommend." (The Environmental Protection Agency has since raised the level to 4 ppm).

As with synthetic chlorine, fluoride is a chemical "wildcat." Fluoride is a byproduct of all large chemical laboratories. Do not confuse sodium fluoride with natural fluoride. *Sodium fluoride is synthetic and poisonous.*

The process of fluoridation arose from the discovery that in a Texas county, the soil contained an abundance of natural fluorine. For this reason, said dentists, there was a low incidence of decay in the teeth of youngsters.

Companies who could not dispose of the synthetic by-product of fluoride and many dentists expressed the controversial opinion that fluoride in tap water would help protect the teeth just as would natural fluorine in the Texas county.

Today, at least 88 million pounds of fluoride are shipped to our water works for eventual human consumption. The greatest users of this deadly poison are municipal water systems, toothpaste companies and the dental profession.

Fluoridation was begun in 1945, based upon a half century of research. But it still is a controversial matter.

Dr. Robert J. H. Mick, a dentist who once actively promoted fluoride, then opposed it, stated, "I was probably one of the first persons in the world to promote fluoridation, until I became interested in body chemistry."

(In 1949, Dr. Mick was appointed an international representative of the American Academy of Nutrition. He conducted experiments with animals on food and fluorides. He conducted studies in Africa, among natives, on the relationship of fluoridated water and foods to dental decay. He also conducted similar studies in the U.S. with children.)

*Health Hazard.* Dr. Mick states, "As a result of experiments with animals we learned that bones, teeth, kidneys, livers and spleens had accumulated up to 50 percent more fluoride than controlled animals. Cripples were born to the third generation."

In other reports, cows became crippled by eating forage containing 97 parts per million of fluorides. They had to graze on their knees. Their backs and necks became so immobilized that they could not stand the agony of bending. Fluorides created this deadly crippling on some animals. It can create a hazard to humans.

*Dental Hazard.* A medical dictionary says about "mottled" teeth: "A chronic endemic dental fluorosis that is found in communities using a drinking water that contains one part or more of fluoride per million [very small]. The permanent teeth of children so raised, tend to erupt more or less chalky white in color, and later tend to become pitted and stained yellow, brown or almost black."

This refers to just one part per million. It is apparent that a buildup in the system can be hazardous to both teeth and body.

### Symptoms of possible fluoride poisoning

The following statement appeared in *The Milwaukee Journal*, Tuesday, June 8, 1971:

Don't get the idea your troubles are imaginary. Very many subjects are told by their physicians that their ailments are caused by nerves. Fluoride can cause both the nerve disorder and the other ailments.

## THE ILL EFFECTS OF FLUORIDE

Tiredness and weakness

Pins and needles sensation

Kidney and bladder disorders

Constipation

Vomiting, especially mucous

Itching after bath

Excessive thirst

Headache

Arthritis

Gum diseases

Nervousness

Diarrhea

Loss of hair

Skin disorders

Stomach disorders

Numbness in hands

Brittle nails                "Charley horse"
Sinus disorders              Mouth ulcers
                             Disturbed vision

If your physician suggests that any of these symptoms are caused by nerves, discuss with him the possibility of fluoride poisoning. Your very first step is to change your drinking water. If the symptoms vanish or you begin to feel better, you can believe that your problems stemmed from fluorides in the water.

Aside from the advantage of removing chlorine, distillation also removes the fluorides from water, a safe method of avoiding the hazards of fluoridation.

## FLUORIDATION ISN'T THAT GREAT

*In May, 1989, after analyzing data from a National Institute of Dental Research survey which examined the teeth of over 40,000 children from 84 different areas around the United States, John Yiamouyiannis, Ph.D., concluded that there is no significant difference in the decay rate of permanent teeth among children living in fluoridated and nonfluoridated areas.*

CHAPTER 10

# *The Effect of Water On Your Kidneys*

An increasing number of people (of all ages, including youngsters) are showing problems with their kidneys. Malfunctioning of the kidneys is a contributing cause to many ailments. When the kidneys fail to filter poisons out of the bloodstream, uremic poisoning can begin and may be fatal.

Properly functioning kidneys are vital. That is why nature gave us two of them. If one falters, another one is handy. Yes, kidneys have been transplanted (especially within a family), but it is sensible to eliminate any possible causes of kidney trouble so that transplants are unnecessary! Nothing man-made can ever replace that which is nature-made. Since the kidneys are so valuable, they should be treated properly.

Basically, the kidneys have a "filtering" system that helps remove toxins and byproducts carried by the blood to the kidneys—much like an oil filter for an automobile. The kidneys eliminate about two quarts of inorganic and some organic salts and acid, including sulphates, calcium, potassium, sodium, magnesium, ammonia, chlorides, uric acid pigments and so on.

Many of these inorganic minerals are taken into the system through the drinking of hard water. Since you cannot assimilate these elements, the kidneys try to eliminate them. But many such minerals are deposited in our tissues, blood vessels, joints, heart valves and nerve centers so they cannot reach the kidneys. Drinking hard water, saturated with inorganic minerals, puts a greater load on the kidneys and may contribute to the formation of kidney stones or gallstones.

Gravel in the body refers to sandy deposits formed in the kidneys and passed in the urine. They are made up of salts of calcium, phosphorus, oxalic and uric acids. If these gravel stones are acid in their formations, then it would be wise to change to alkaline foods and of course, to pure water which has an alkaline pH factor.

Calcification can appear in patches all over the body. Cases have been reported in which calcified lumps the size of an egg may form in a muscle. Lime salts begin as gravel in the kidneys and bladder. If these are noticed in the urine, precautions should be taken against stone formations. You then need to examine the type of water you are drinking.

Since hard water is the recognized chief culprit in carrying inorganic minerals into the system, distilled water will help stop this problem and will also help to dissolve the inorganic minerals already clogging up the system.

It is important to note that kidney machines use distilled water. Fluorides are taboo because they can be fatal. In one reported situation, the use of fluoridated city water in artificial kidney machines contributed to the problem of bone disease, spontaneous fractures, weak muscles, nerve irritation and a vague metabolic disorder.

Similar cases were reported wherein fluoridated tap water was used in kidney machines with very distressing results. This knowledge has now been passed on to all doctors using such kidney machines. They are now alerted to this problem.

When we can help dissolve the hard water film which clogs up our cells and organs, we can be hopeful for better health.

*Case Reports.* "Mrs. J. O., about 22 years of age, was a recent medical patient, troubled with kidney and bladder disorders, and with excessive tiredness and nervousness. She wondered whether these ill effects could be caused by fluoride. After avoiding fluoridated water for a brief period, her kidney trouble and other symptoms vanished. Her husband, who was also adversely affected by fluoride, recovered in the same manner." (*Milwaukee Journal,* June 8, 1971.)

While this may be a speedy cure, and the cumulative effects will still have to be filtered out of Mrs. J. O.'s system, it does prove that fluoridated and chemicalized water can be contradictory to good health.

It is possible that when a newborn child cries until its face is blue, a bottle of pure water would be all that is needed to soothe the child to a restful sleep!

In 1965, the University of Rochester cautioned against the use of fluoridated water in artificial kidney therapy. But health officials disregarded the warning. Only when it resulted in a catastrophe, with 21 out of 21 patients seriously harmed, was the practice stopped.

Mrs. E. M., an elderly lady, suffered from unendurable headaches, kidney and bladder disorders and a host of other ills. Her son manifested typical symptoms of fluoride illness and had been hospitalized five times. Both mother and son would habitually over-drink large amounts of water. It was told to me that when they *avoided* fluoridated water, their illnesses disappeared, especially their kidney and bladder problems.

As long as there are poisons and toxins in our systems, it is essential to use pure water as the most potent (and most natural) way to get rid of them.

Kidneys need water—the best water. A deficiency of *pure* drinking water contributes to problems of faulty oxidation, poor dissolution and inadequate flushing out of waste products from the kidneys.

A glass or two of pure water before a meal should help furnish enough solvent liquid to help the kidneys remove the toxins from body tissues.

Pure water can also help dissolve mineral deposits on the minute network of tubules and capillaries that circulate the bloodstream of the body continuously.

Healthy kidneys also help remove excess water from the bloodstream, thus keeping this vital fluid at the proper concentration every moment of life. Your kidneys are among your most important organs. Take care of them.

## LOOKS CAN BE DECEIVING

*We already know that just because a glass of water looks clear, it is no assurance that it is pure. The only way to get this assurance is to distill the water which helps to eliminate inorganic minerals and chemicals that could be harmful to the kidneys and the rest of the body.*

# CHAPTER 11

# Pure Water and Arthritis

Arthritis is a disease that has plagued humanity for thousands of years. Many disinterred skeletons show the ravages of gnarled and deformed bones. Some label it as an "aging disease." But this is questionable since youngsters, too, have arthritis. It may well be a disease of erroneous living.

Most people have arthritis to some degree. A child's joints may be so supple that they appear to be jointless. By the time a child reaches the age of 20, the joints become quite set. Stiffness shows up with each exertion. This is considered a form of arthritis.

As the years advance, the pattern of walking, stopping and turning becomes set. Agility may decline. In many such situations, a form of arthritis has taken hold. It is believed that 9 out of every 10 of our older citizens have arthritis in one form or another.

Is there a cure for arthritis? Medical science says, "No!" You are told to live with your disease. So far, the only remedy recommended is aspirin or other pain pills. Bones still will become articulated to each other at the joints. Inflamed and stiffened condition of these joints prevents freedom of movement.

There are over 100 different types of arthritis listed; they vary with the individual. Still, most are classified as stiff and swelling joints.

As inorganic mineral deposits settle in the joints, they become crystal sharp. As the joints move, an irritation is set up. This causes pain or swelling. The more pain, the less movement. The less movement, the more the deposits. This results in a chronic irritation of these structures leading often to the formation of calcified and fibrotic deposits causing spasm and wasting of muscles, immobility of joints, accompanied by unbearable pulling, pinching and shooting pains. Extra amounts of calcium, normally removed from the blood and eliminated, are deposited instead in the joints, causing bursas (known as bursitis) on the ends of the bones and in the muscles. Here they cause great pressure on nerves, giving rise to the most excruciating pains, besides crippling the structures affected.

Since this crippling ailment strikes almost everyone, there are many theories as to the cause. One suggestion is that it can be traced to the type of hard water we drink.

Hard water has existed since the beginning of time. Any water that runs over rocks and seeps into the ground becomes hard. One writer says that hard water dissolves the metal in nails, which, of course, it does via oxidation. *Water is a solvent and designed to do just that!* However, it has taken us a long time to discover that the only avenue inorganic minerals take into our bodies is through the hard water we drink.

Farmers get their inorganic minerals from deep well water. City people get their inorganic minerals from tap water, together with chlorine, fluorides and other chemicals. Water is always dissolving as it travels. If it is not contaminated from our ground, it is from the water mains in cities. Often, water travels through miles of water mains before it reaches your tap. By that time, it is well saturated with metals and chemicals.

Arthritis is not the only problem caused by the hardness in our water. Many other problems may also be related. For example, hardening of the arteries, diabetes, gallstones, kidney stones, cataracts, loss of hearing, loss of memory, are all related to premature aging, and the causes can be allied to water hardness.

Here is a letter written to me:

Several months ago, we obtained a water distiller. After only two months of use, my wife began to feel better and more energetic.

Previously she complained regularly of aching and stiffness in her joints, particularly in the knees and hips. After three months on distilled water, these complaints are all but forgotten and she would not think of being without distilled water.

As for myself, I was, during this time, recovering from a minor wrench of a knee and withheld any comment on its effect.

I can certify, and so do, that my joints are free of the old stiffness and I can bend my knees freely now, and we both know that it is due to drinking water and furthermore, no other treatment, remedy or exercise was in any way implemented during this time.

C.A.S., Sioux City, Iowa

Another man wrote, "I had been taking pain pills regularly for arthritis. I have had no shots during the six months I have used my home water distiller."

Many people are asking if pure water can completely rid their bodies of arthritis. The answer is that it cannot *completely* cast out arthritis. It has taken years to accumulate inorganic minerals in the tissues and joints. Logically, it should take much time to remove all these deposits. Personally, my opinion is that if distilled water is used during the entire lifetime, the joints should be reasonably free of deposits.

Physicians agree that pain keeps you from harming yourself with active exercise. Nothing keeps you from doing harm with too much rest. Yet, the proper amount of rest is as important as physical activity.

The lining of a badly inflamed joint is harsh. Moving the joint rubs roughened surfaces together and causes further irritation. You often have to move a joint enough to keep it from getting stiff. This is a calculated risk. An uncomfortable joint can be used to the limit of your comfort. But a reddened, swollen and hot joint deserves rest. It should be moved only in deliberate, motion-saving exercises.

If you use pure water, the mineral deposits around the joints gradually become chalky as they soften.

The first thing you notice is that your joints will move more freely because the sharp crystals lose their sharp peaks. By applying heat, more blood is drawn to the inflamed joint. A gentle massage (toward the heart) will help distribute the dissolved mineral salts, so that they can be carried away by the bloodstream.

Arthritics should guard against tension. When the mind is tense, the muscle fibers contract, squeezing the blood vessels. This constricts the blood flow to that particular area, resulting in an under-supply of oxygen and a lessened outflow of toxins and wastes.

At the same time, some other area or organ is over-gorged with blood. The results in both cases are equally bad. There should not be any imbalance in blood flow. It should be equal in all directions. Relaxation is important for the improvement of the health of arthritics and others.

It is important to eat as many raw foods as possible. A vegetable juicer and a good blender are most essential. Raw fruits and raw vegetables are known as "live" foods. They contain all their enzymes and minerals.

### A chiropractor writes

As a practicing chiropractor for thirty-one years, it was a constant observation of mine that of the many factors determining the degree of one's health quotient, in the anabolic sense, the quality and quantity of water was foremost.

Having used spring water exclusively for twenty-five years and distilled water for only two weeks, "the choice is clearer than clear"! What a difference in my own body. Please let me know where and how I can obtain a worthwhile distilling unit.

E.J.B., Washington, D. C.

### Freedom from pain

A friend of mine, Vincent L. in Vermont, told me about the importance of drinking good water in order to enjoy good health. I decided to do something. Not having a home distiller at the time, I purchased "distilled water" from our local drugstore. After reading the fine print on the label, I discovered it was "de-ionized" which I knew you did not recommend.

After purchasing my own distiller, I soon found that it lessened stiffness in my back and muscles.

I think that having pure water is like "nectar from Heaven" and I only wish I could have known about it years ago. Dr. Banik, I started getting lame in 1967. Now I can walk only with the aid of two canes. I've never given up. Now, I know why. I cannot tell you how wonderful it is to feel less pain and to be less lame in such a short while.

Please send me more information on water, so I can spread the news far and wide. May God bless you with His abundance of whatever you require in your great service.

Mrs. J.W., Mabalia, Calif.

Arthritis is no simple disease. There is no definite way of either acquiring arthritis or curing it. There are many remedies and proposed cures among the different healing professions. One point is certain— no matter what the suggestions for a cure, or the procedure required—distilled water should play a most important part of the treatment.

## THE BENEFITS OF GLACIER WATER

*People living in high mountains, who generally drink glacier or snow water, have less arthritis and reportedly enjoy longer life spans than those who drink hardened water from the city.*

# Chapter 12

# Pure Water and Allergies, Diabetes

Nearly every person at one time or another, knowingly or unknowingly, is afflicted with allergies. If you suffer from even one small allergy, you feel miserable!

The symptoms of allergies are as varied as hives, hay fever, nausea, vomiting, headaches, skin rash, eczema, asthma, hoarseness and so on. The list is endless. It is all according to individual body chemistry.

Research is currently underway to determine the effect that distilled water may have on allergies. But we already know one thing. Long-lived people do not appear to have many allergies.

### Pure water and diabetes

You will know if you have diabetes. Of course, it is wise to obtain regular physical examinations by your doctor, rather than wait until the onset of the ailment. But generally speaking, diabetes is characterized by excessive thirst and urination, usually caused by an unreasonable, excessive devouring of carbohydrates in the form of pies, cakes, ice cream, candy, sweet drinks or anything high in sugar and starches.

Starches turn into sugars. It is then the function of the pancreas, which produces natural insulin, to neutralize the sugar. If the pancreas fails to produce enough insulin, an oversupply of sugar is secreted in the bloodstream. Hence the name, "insulin," or a synthetic hormone to neutralize the sugar.

The diabetic usually feels dry in the mouth and throat and his thirst for water is extreme. His appetite is poor. He usually loses weight, although at first he may seem to hold his weight.

Diabetics are not all fat. Many slim people who consume very little sugar and carbohydrates also become diabetic. A clue here is the cause of this ailment. Within the deeper layer of the epidermis of the pancreas lie the cells of Langerhans. These cells produce needed insulin. But—while these cells may not die, they often just fail to function. Why? Some doctors believe that they are clogged by excess mineral deposits and their action is impaired.

If this is true, then it is important to consider the intake of pure water, which is known to help dissolve such deposits. The cells of Langerhans could then be free to produce sufficient insulin to neutralize the excessive sugar.

For example, Z.A.S., a mechanic, had diabetes so badly that both of his feet were numb. One day he dropped a heavy tool on his foot. That night he removed his shoes. One shoe was partially filled with blood. His father (age 84) had received so much relief from arthritis by drinking pure water, that he suggested his son try it. He said it would surely help his diabetes. The son followed his father's advice. In less than two weeks of drinking pure water, the numbness left his feet. He was able to go back to work. He still finds it difficult to believe that such relief could occur in such a short time.

## NATURAL vs. PURE

*We think of water from natural springs as being pure and beneficial to health, but the reverse is often true. For example, the springs feeding the Arkansas and Red River carry seventeen tons of salt per minute. New Mexico's Lemonade Springs have a high content of sulfuric acid. And Colorado's Asure Yampah Spring has eight times more radium than the Public Health Service sets as a safe limit.*

# CHAPTER 13

## Pure Water and Premature Aging

It is believed that a factor contributing to premature old age is the calcareous lime or earthy deposits which accumulate in the body. Many believe that what we term "old age" is actually a condition partially brought about by the body becoming ossified from these calcareous deposits, which slowly but continuously occur throughout the body. In order to help delay or prevent early aging, it is necessary to protect the body against these lime deposits for as long as possible.

It is said that man begins in a gelatinous state and ends in an osseous or bony condition. From the moment of birth, there is a gradual process of ossification. But after passing middle life, the ossifying tendency becomes more markedly developed, until it finally can become senile decrepitude.

These hard deposits interfere with the free performance of the functioning of the organs. In turn, this leads to imperfect circulation. The heart gradually toughens. The large blood vessels become blocked up by calcareous matter. Nutrition and metabolism become hindered.

You can easily test the matter of calcareous deposit in water by a simple experiment using an ordinary tea kettle. After it has been used for some time, empty it. Now place the empty kettle on the back of the stove to thoroughly dry the accumulated minerals so that it will become brittle. Then with a wooden object tap the sides and bottom of the kettle in order to dislodge the calcareous substances clinging to the inside of the kettle. Remove the scale thus dislodged and examine it.

The average tea kettle does not evaporate a very great amount of water. Yet there is conclusive evidence of a continual accumulation of these calcareous deposits.

This is further shown by the accumulation of "scale" in the average steam boiler, as well as in the average automobile radiator, both of which have to be repeatedly cleansed in order to perform their work properly.

From this, we see that there are two ways in which such calcareous matters are introduced into the body. First through the medium of some of the food we eat. Secondly, in the water we drink.

The use of pure water for drinking and cooking can minimize or prevent this difficulty.

Distilled water is that which has been purified by a process of artificial evaporation and subsequent condensation. The vapor is cooled and turned back into water again. This makes it impossible for the lime, the stone, the sand, the dirt or any of the impurities to be carried off into the steam. All such foreign matter remains in the bottom of the still or kettle, leaving the condensation safe, pure and wholesome.

The cloud which issues from the spout of the tea kettle and which we commonly call "steam," really consists of tiny droplets of distilled water. Anyone examining this so-called steam as it leaves the spout of a kettle in which the water has been rapidly boiled, will see a little gap between the cloud and the spout. This gap is really filled with the invisible water vapor which, as fast as it gets into the atmosphere, becomes cool and is changed back into liquid water.

It may therefore be seen how completely purifying is the process of distillation. Microorganisms, dead organic matter and mineral matter must all remain behind in the water left in the tea kettle or in the still. They cannot be held and carried over to the "cloud" by an invisible gas.

One time, while at a country home, our water system went wrong early one morning. Upon arising, I found no water with which to wash.

But I did have a two-gallon bottle of distilled water in my bathroom, and I used that for washing my face and hands. Throughout the day, I noticed how soft and smooth my skin was. No doubt, this was due to the water I had used.

If pure, soft, distilled water will have this effect upon the usually rough skin of a man's face and hands, what will it do to the soft, delicate membrane lining of the interior of the body?

The minerals in ordinary drinking water act as irritant toxins. But distilled water is pure. That is what the body needs—instead of water with inorganic minerals, clay, limestone, and all manner of animal, vegetable and mineral debris which the kidneys must try to eliminate.

As you begin using pure water, you not only help remove much irritation from the kidneys but you increase the purity of the bloodstream and thereby aid in strengthening not only the kidneys but most body organs.

In one reported situation, a woman was troubled with Bright's disease. (This is a disorder of the kidney associated with retention of water in the body causing edema.) She had been unable to lie down for weeks because of feeble heart action and difficulty in breathing. Her pulse was weak (40 beats to the minute) and almost indiscernible at the wrist. She had a bloated abdomen. Her legs were so swollen, the skin cracked open exuding liquid; this meant that her legs had to be constantly wrapped in cloths which demanded constant changing. She was passing less than a pint of urine a day which tests showed to be almost solid albumen.

The woman had undergone much medication, but after months of treatment she was so weak that she was not expected to live.

Another consultant was called on her case, and he immediately put her on a special fast. She was to drink over two quarts of distilled water each day.

Within thirty-six hours, she began to pass three quarts of urine a day. Soon, the bloating lessened. Her heart (almost drowned in the dropsical effusion) became stronger. She began to breathe better. She could soon lie down comfortably in bed and from then on her improvement was progressive.

Pure water thus gave this woman destined to die a new lease on life. It may well be a missing link in the quest for eternal youth.

Pure water has a good taste, unlike ordinary water, which often tastes flat, insipid and sometimes muddy. The insides of the body may look as coated as the inside of a tea kettle. Examine ordinary drinking water with a powerful microscope and you will see each bit of dirt, sand, lime and corrosive minerals. Small wonder that the kidneys become inflamed as they try to strain out all of these impurities.

It takes you only a moment to drink a glass of water. But it forces your kidneys to work ceaselessly, day and night, asleep or awake, to strain out these foreign bodies. If they succeed, they become worn out or inflamed. But if they fail, you see the effects throughout your body in the form of thickened joints, painful nerves, weakened arteries, valvular ailments of the heart, rheumatism and various circulatory disturbances. But distilled water gives the kidneys *no* straining to do because it is pure and helps dissolve away the deposits previously formed, thus both preventing and relieving ailments.

Be on guard to avoid making the interior of your body into a stone quarry. Drinking ordinary hard water can deposit minerals, lime, dissolved stone and corrosive minerals in your system.

## FROM CLOUDS TO YOUR FAUCET

*In its long journey from the clouds to the faucet, water picks up, or dissolves, a little bit of almost everything it touches. Air seems cleaner and fresher after a rain because rain water literally washes the air, gathering dust, fumes and tiny living organisms.*

*Coursing over the earth's surface, water often becomes turbid, or cloudy, as it gathers solid impurities such as silt, sand, mud and clay. Water can become colored as it flows through swamp areas and may also acquire objectionable tastes, and odors from decaying plant and animal life.*

*As water flows over the surface of the earth and seeps into the ground, it dissolves additional impurities such as hardness, iron and many other inorganic minerals. All these are natural water pollutants and can cause water problems in the home and industry.*

# CHAPTER 14

# Little-Known Benefits of Pure Water

There are many rewards for drinking distilled water; these may be relatively unknown. Here are several of them.

### Zinc for sexual growth

Zinc, the mineral, has been said to be helpful for sexual growth. A zinc deficiency may well be the cause of such sex problems as impotence, premature ejaculation, dwarfed sex organs. We do know that small amounts of zinc are helpful for problems of hypertension, testicular atrophy, delayed healing, impaired growth.

But this does not mean the zinc found in drinking water. A medical dictionary tells us that melted zinc, when poured into water, becomes granular in form. Its salts are poisonous. Often, when absorbed by the system, it produces a chronic poisoning resembling that caused by lead.

Zinc is related to cadmium, derived from galvanized plumbing. Cadmium is defined as a bivalent metal, not unlike zinc in appearance and properties. Its salts are said to be poisonous.

(Bivalent means having a valence of two; representing or composed of two homologous chromosomes joined end to end or associated in pairs.)

This suggests an inter-relationship between two poisons—zinc and cadmium. Zinc, in trace amounts, causes similar symptoms of deadly lead poisoning.

We get most of our zinc from water that runs off zinc mines, chemical fertilizers or galvanized plumbing, which often finds its way into our tap water. The tap water we drink carries those poisonous metals in their inorganic state.

Yes, zinc is an important mineral—but NOT chemicalized zinc.

Whenever you galvanize iron water mains, you release zinc and cadmium. These could very well be the elements which cause heart attacks in soft water areas.

To get enough zinc properly it should be taken in an organic form, from the food we eat or from supplements, not in an inorganic state in drinking water. This is another reason why we should drink distilled water so that it is free of such poisons.

*Zinc sources:* In natural foods such as sunflower seeds, squash, pumpkin seeds, bran, wheat germ, whole wheat, millet and old-fashioned rolled oats. Add vitamin E to your diet for more zinc and other nutrients, giving yourself increasing vigor.

### Be careful about salt

Salt is used too freely in cooking. It is regarded as a hazardous compound. Salt is inorganic. True, your body needs some salt, but again only in its organic state. Salt from vegetables and seafoods is high in organic elements. Your tissues can absorb this kind and amount of salt much more easily than from the salt shaker or tap water.

Excessive salt intake calls for more water to wash away the accumulated calcium chloride. You then consume more salt which triggers a craving for still more water. The vicious cycle grows. If you find yourself drinking excessive amounts of water during a meal (and after), you may have consumed excessive salt. Heavy liquid drinkers are great salt users.

Many of the canned soups, vegetables, cold meats and restaurant foods are heavily salted. If you are on a reducing diet, cut down on salt. When eating out, specify no salt in your foods. You may try kelp or sea salt (sold at all health stores and many supermarkets) to give good minerals to your system and a taste of salt, the natural way.

Use any salt most sparingly. Salt waterlogs

your tissues and cells, often imprisoning up to a gallon of water, which is 8.33 pounds. So be moderate in the use of any salt.

A housewife wrote to the Office of Saline Water, U.S. Department of the Interior, to say that she noticed the water that condensed on the lid of a pan while she was cooking was not salty. Why not use this discovery to help ease the nation's water problems? she asked. This is precisely the most popular method of desalting —by distillation or evaporation, where the overhead steam is condensed and the salt is left behind as a by-product. The housewife had not invented this process, but the Office of Saline Water thanked her just the same.

Today, many of our coastal cities, and even far-inland cities, suffer from high salt concentrations in their water. At least some 1,000 cities have concentrations of salt up to 1.5 percent (oceans 3.5 percent). We adapt to salt, much as we adapt to any other drug or chemical. Gradually, we can absorb more and more, not realizing why something wrong is happening to our bodies.

People who eat highly salted foods such as salted peanuts, soda crackers, salted popcorn, canned soups, and many other processed foods have many resulting problems. The solution lies in avoiding these salty foods, eating wholesome, natural foods and drinking distilled, salt-free water.

Most tap water has an unusual amount of salt. If you are concerned about better health (and who isn't?), then drink salt-free distilled water and give your body working material out of which may be fashioned robust good health!

### Keeping yourself young

If you notice a decline in activity and energy even in your early twenties, it suggests that your body has accumulated much waste. The joy of movement is impeded. In old age, every cell may be so loaded that it is *impossible* to move with ease and skill; still more impossible to move with the joy and buoyancy of youth.

In later life, cells may be encased in calcium shells. They may also be separated from one another by walls of poisonous waste matter. This reduces the energy supply for nerve cells and muscles; only enough is there to allow some motion without surplus enjoyment. The body may then arrive at the "stone age."

Heart attacks and hardening of the arteries are our nation's number one killer. Calcium deposits along the artery wall tend to harden the arteries until they lose elasticity. Under sudden exertion or excitement, the vessels rupture. X rays reveal these deposits very clearly. Vessels clogged with calcium are also clearly visible on the retina, showing up as small and silvery. An eye specialist can predict hardening of the arteries years in advance. While hardening of the arteries is not necessarily fatal, it does threaten optimum health. Tap water may cause these deposits on the arteries.

Calcium deposits take place anywhere in the body, whether it be in the joints or along the arteries. Even heart valves reveal deposits up to 0.18 of an inch thick. There are cases on record wherein such mineral deposits have been removed or dissolved by drinking distilled water.

It is not necessarily what we *put into* the water that is so vital. It is what we *take out* that really matters. If it takes years to build up these deposits, it will take time to remove them. It is wise to keep the body free of deposits beginning as early in life as possible. It is never too late to begin doing so . . . neither is it ever too early!

Only the purest of all waters should enter our systems. We put the best fuels and oils into our cars, yet we put the worst kinds of water in our bodies.

Before you drink tap water, hold it to the light and tell yourself, "Along with this water I may be drinking arsenic, iron, manganese, copper, zinc, radium and who knows what else?"

*You Do Need Minerals.* These should be organic and from fruits, vegetables, grains and other wholesome, natural foods. This is the healthy way to feed *organic* minerals to your body as opposed to the *inorganic* sludge-type minerals in tap water.

When you use pure water, you and your family will experience a new feeling of vitality. Use it for making tea and soups and for all cooking. Drink several glasses throughout the day. It helps keep you cleansed, inside and outside.

If there is one rule of health, it should be, "Drink ye freely of the water of life!"

Simple proof of the benefits of good water can be seen in our green fields and pastures. If rain water is good for plants, distilled water, which is the equivalent of rain water purified of pollutants, is good for humans. This is the way to keep inorganic mineral deposits out of the body. The body is designed to retain and use desirable nutrients and expel the elements that cannot be accommodated in proper functioning.

Think again of the best proof of the quality of tap water—your grandmother's tea kettle. Ask yourself, do you want to drink the sludge collected on the bottom or do you want to drink the steam which spouted out of the tea kettle? This steam, condensed, is your rain water purified. It is the purest water you can drink.

A small home distiller is one way to provide yourself with pure water every day of your long and healthy life. All you need to do is plug the cord into a light socket. In a few hours (depending on the size of the distiller you have), you will have a gallon of refreshing, pure water.

Meanwhile join local groups to help combat increasing water pollution in your area. Get all the material you can from the Environmental Protection Agency. Study it carefully. Because as we begin adding miles and miles of underground waterways, continue getting our drinking water from polluted lakes and rivers and deep wells and continue adding chlorine and fluorides to "decontaminate" our water, our death rate of many diseases now begins to strike among the very young. Even babies in cribs are victims. Isn't it about time we think of the real issue? True, water is not the only cause. We need to think of all pollutants. So far, we have one answer to water pollution. It is the best answer—distillation. This we can accomplish overnight with a home distiller. Until the water in our lakes, rivers and oceans can become pure again, will we be able to enjoy a glass of water and have the positive assurance that the water is fit to drink for our innocent children and ourselves? The purpose of this book is to tell you many things about the water you drink—its possible merits and its lurking dangers. All of it is invisible—its effects are visible! As this book leaves the publisher's shelves, it will have a life of its own. It will meet with oppositions and it will be welcomed with joy. Some will throw the book aside—others will cherish its teachings. To you, who have stayed with me until now, I commend your loyalty and ask for your friendship. I need you to tell others—so others can tell others. Only then can we say "Well done!"

# PURE WATER—DOES IT EXIST?

*No new water is ever created in nature, it is only recycled. Rain is, in effect, distilled water which has evaporated from the oceans and rivers, from the plants and soil—cooled, formed clouds—and fallen once again on the earth. Nature, in this way, can purify a fixed supply of water. Today, rain becomes polluted even before it reaches the ground. The increasing demands on this finite water supply are so great that roughly one out of every two people in North America is drinking processed sewer water. As a matter of fact, the government has judged that a mere 40 percent of sewage treatment systems in the nation are adequate.*

# CHAPTER 15

# Some Questions and Answers About Pure Water

Through the years, because of my interest in the subject, and because of the wide circulation of my book, *The Choice Is Clear,* I have received hundreds of inquiries about the subject of water—polluted and pure. Here is a random sampling of them, and my answers.

1. *How much water shall I drink?*

The National Research Council suggests ten to eleven glasses daily for adults. Other authorities recommend six to eight glasses daily. Much of this water we get in foods and vegetables. Water is essential to us for the elimination of waste from the body, and the freer and more active our circulation, the more readily are injurious substances removed. I try to drink two to four glasses per hour for short periods of time, during hot days, believing that it is always better to drink more, rather than less, water.

2. *Is spring or mineral water pure water?*

No. It is merely taken out of a spring, tap or well, with all the usual pollutants present.

3. *Can a municipal water supply become contaminated?*

Certainly—and it is happening more and more frequently today, not only with dangerous minerals but also with human waste. The U.S. Public Health Service report contains facts on this.

4. *Can you get seriously ill from drinking contaminated water?*

Yes, many doctors having written and talked on this subject, giving evidence that water, contaminated with human excrement, has caused cholera and other epidemics occurring in many areas of the earth. These same conditions exist today and such epidemics are even more prevalent.

5. *Aside from municipal water supplies, what is the other normal source of drinking water?*

Wells are the major source; and these can be very dangerous especially when located on small plots, where it is almost impossible to keep the seepage from the cesspool or septic tank out of such wells.

6. *How long will it take to correct water pollution in the United States?*

Some authorities say it will take ten years; others say one hundred years. The facts are that the U.S. Public Health Service reports show that practically every river and lake in our country is contaminated, many with very dangerous pollution.

7. *What is your opinion of bottled water?*

Bottled water is marketed today under many different labels—and the labels often reveal the ignorance of the bottler. Some labels identify their product as "spring-like," "filtered," "mountain-fresh," "electrified," "mineralized," or "de-ionized." These descriptions are meaningless in most instances. It is interesting to note that the Consumer Bulletin (Page 32, January, 1973), reported that the Supreme Court had canceled its contract for delivery of bottled water, apparently convinced by a report from researchers at Georgetown University. Many brands may not be safe to drink. According to this research, only one brand was bacteria-free; three other brands had more bacteria than local tap water. Actually, the Federal government has no standards for drinking water except the water which is supplied through municipal water systems.

8. *Do water softeners purify water?*

Water softeners do not purify water in any sense of the word, as a matter of fact, the majority of them are water contaminators. It has been proved that water softeners do not kill bacteria or remove mineral impurities, but merely add additional salts to the water since this water treatment is based on a salt-operated unit.

9. *What is the process of distilling water?*

It is the process by which ordinary tap water is first heated to the boiling point so that impurities are separated out from the water, which, itself becomes vapor or steam. The resulting vapor is then rapidly cooled and converted back into pure or refined water. The impurities remain in the residue which is simply thrown away.

10. *What is single distilled water?*

Water run through a distiller once is considered single distilled. It is about 99 percent plus pure. Quite often, for laboratory needs, distilled water is re-distilled several times. Single distilled water is more than amply pure for drinking purposes.

11. *Is such distilled water good for you to drink?*

In my opinion, it is the most healthful, purest water you can drink.

12. *Why do you say this? What proof have you?*

Let's begin with the fact that the entire U.S. Navy drinks distilled water when aboard ship—via a distillation unit which converts sea water to pure distilled water. Furthermore, patients on sodium restricted diets are advised to drink only distilled water. The United States Public Health Service, after a great deal of testing, recommended distilled water to their various clinics as did the Duke Medical Center.

13. *Why do you believe distilled water is best for cooking?*

Distilled water adds no foreign substances to your food. The original tastes and flavors of your food are preserved.

14. *Why is this water so pure?*

The distillation process boils the source water, collects the resulting steam, cools and condenses it back into the water. Bacteria and germs are immediately killed by the heat of the steam. Salts, sulfur, arsenic, mercury, chlorine and other chemicals impurities do not boil at the same temperature as the water. They do not therefore become steam, and do not travel into the cooling, condensing apparatus of the distiller.

15. *What about the minerals removed from water by this process? Don't we need them?*

As you no doubt know by now, distillation removes all minerals, including the good ones like calcium and magnesium. We must have minerals to maintain optimum health. For those who do not get the proper amount of minerals from fruits, vegetables, seeds, nuts, meats, dairy products, wholegrains, etc., it may be necessary to take vitamin and mineral supplements, which are available at health food stores and other outlets.

16. *Are there any other methods of getting 100 percent pure water?*

No. While they may help somewhat, filters, reverse osmosis, electrodialysis, ultraviolet ray and other methods cannot give you 100 percent pure water.

17. *Is there any other way of purifying contaminated water?*

Yes, but only one other sure way—by chlorination. The disadvantage of chlorination, as U.S. Public Health Service reports show, is the extreme difficulty in handling and in maintaining the right proportions. Furthermore, chlorination may add a very disagreeable taste to the water. And lastly, in the form it is put into water, it is a cumulative poison; many doctors believe that chlorine is a contributing factor in atherosclerosis.

## FIGHT POLLUTION

*There are numerous anti-pollution organizations in the nation that are making progress in the campaign against pollution. These conservation groups recognize the urgency of combat-*

*ing water, air and land pollution and providing
a more livable environment. In your own community and region, these groups deserve your
all-out cooperation and support.*

## Would You Like to Feel Wonderful? Here Is the Secret!

Today there is great concern about the kind of water we should drink. Shall we filter it, demineralize it, electrify it, boil it, de-ionize it, fortify it, steam distill it—or just drink it from the tap? Perhaps the following testimonial from Jared Looser, Salt Lake City, Utah, may clarify the problem.

"As a paraplegic with my bladder catheterized, I had to drink quantities of liquids. I usually drank herb teas, water, fruit and vegetable juices. My doctor told me to keep my bladder and kidneys 'running.'

"I soon realized I was a candidate for bladder stones, no matter how careful I was. Medication used to work for a few weeks at a time, but then my body would rebel and build up a resistance. I tried all kinds of different waters. First I used well water. However, I had to return to the hospital to have two bladder stones the size of chicken eggs taken out. This is *not* exaggerated. They were just that large.

"After surgery, I switched to bottled spring water, but this too formed a stony crust—like eggshells around the catheter. Time after time, I had to return to my doctor to have my bladder flushed. Sometimes he had to crush the eggshells to flush the bladder. This was very painful.

"I then decided to install a water softener. It formed the same crust. Several months later I was told that our local spring water company was the best. I bought twelve gallons. Again, that did not solve my problem. I had to be catheterized more frequently.

"Last March, my mother returned from her chiropractor with your book, *The Choice Is Clear*. She told me that Dr. Benson drank *steam distilled* water, and offered her a drink. She said, 'I've never tasted such delicious, clean water.'

"I then concentrated on your book. I immediately bought a large water distiller, and what a joy to drink the first bubbling glass of distilled water. And after having used this distilled water for only two days, my urine was astonishingly clean and sand free, and it has been so ever since. Before, I had to change the catheter every day for cleaning and re-sterilizing. Now, at the end of four days, it is still very clean.

"Dr. Banik, I feel better all over, and know I

will walk again. Some day I'll come out to visit you. It will be the greatest event in my life. I have written this letter with gratitude in my heart."

JARED LOOSER

We now understand why hospitals used *distilled water* in their kidney machines (Hemodialysis). Kidneys cannot function if their delicate screening system is congested with inorganic minerals.

\* \*

Every baseball player, young or old, knows the story of Connie Mack. The late Emmett Culligan, the greatest name in water, relates his experience with Mr. Mack:

"Several years ago at a hotel in Ft. Lauderdale [Mrs. Culligan and I] walked past a great pile of crated five-gallon bottles stacked three high and for some fifty feet. I asked the bell boy 'What is all this water doing here?' He answered, 'Them is Connie Mack's. He has his team here for Spring practice. He insists that his ball players drink nothing but glacier water. Our Florida water ain't good enough.'

"The next morning Connie and I were in the lobby awaiting 6:30 breakfast. I said to him, 'Mr. Mack, I am a water man. Your mountain water intrigues me. What is the story behind it?'

"He answered, 'Well, my son, in the early days my greatest trouble was in regulating the bowels and stiff shoulders of my team. This condition would break out with any one of my men. At one location where we would visit several times a year, about half of the team would be in trouble. Back in Philadelphia I consulted a doctor. He told me, 'You can expect this ailment when your team drinks different waters wherever you go.' He advised the only way to solve the problem would be to provide the men all season with the same water. That fall, Mrs. Mack and I took the train west to Glacier National Park. The first morning at breakfast we drank the finest water I ever tasted. We were told it came fresh from the melted glaciers.

" 'I made arrangements to have the water bottled and shipments scheduled to meet our team wherever we traveled the following season. This practice became routine for thirty years. From that day to this, I have had no bowel disorders, nor did my team have sore shoulders.' "

Mr. Mack died at the age of 93. He attended baseball games to the very end. What Mr. Mack did not realize was that glacier water checks out as *single distilled* water.

The late Dr. Charles Mayo, one of the two founders of the famous Mayo Clinic, had this to say about water and its mineral content: "Most mineral-laden waters are constipating. Glacier water is super-saturated with dissolved oxygen and also carries the radiated energy of the sun—which we now understand to be natural atomic energy. [It is] low in inorganic minerals. Water hardness is inorganic minerals in solution."

We should feel grateful to Jared Looser, whose discovery of distilled water for paraplegics may save many lives. As for Emmett Culligan and Connie Mack—there are none greater. They deserve a place in the Hall of Fame.

In conclusion, let me say we do not live alone, neither do we work alone. Only by the combined efforts towards a common cause can we move the mountain before us.

ALLEN E. BANIK, O.D.

# Three New Books About

## CANDIDA ALBICANS: A TWENTIETH CENTURY DISEASE

☐ **1. The Candida Albicans Yeast-Free Cookbook
by Pat Connolly    $9.95**

The official cookbook of the Price-Pottenger Nutrition Foundation, written to answer requests for information from more then 75,000 Candida sufferers. Everything you need to know about meal planning, forbidden foods and how to change eating habits to rid yourself of yeast-related disease. Includes the famous ''Rainbow meal plan,'' a menu sampler and a Candida questionnaire.

☐ **2. Candida: A Twentieth–Century Disease
by Shirley Lorenzani, Ph.D. $3.95**

Candidiasis, a major illness of our time, has found a clear helpful exposition of its causes, effect and means of cure in this new book by a health practioner and author who has lived through it.

☐ **3. Candida Albicans: A Health Guide
by Ray Wunderlich, M.D. and Dwight K. Kalita, Ph.D.    $1.95**

An inexpensive Candida primer — how to fight an exploding epidemic of yeast-related diseases. Learn how to prevent an attack by upgrading your nutritional intake, using proper nutrients and a carefully controlled diet.